EARLY PRAISE FOR MINYAN

"A thoughtful, realistic, and authentically Jewish guide, this book has the power to change people's lives."

HAROLD KUSHNER,
author of *When Bad Things Happen to Good People*

"Rami Shapiro brings a fresh new approach to the practice of meditation in a Jewish spiritual context. His warmth of heart and dedication to applying the fruits of his insight are manifest on every page. *Minyan* is a welcome addition to the exciting Jewish renewal movement."

PERLE BESSERMAN,
author of *The Way of the Jewish Mystics*

"This book can show American Jews how to begin the search for their own interior spirituality. Rabbi Shapiro not only illuminates the heart of Judaism's ethical laws and rituals, he offers a new kind of guidance for putting them into practice."

JACOB NEEDLEMAN,
author of *The Heart of Philosophy*

Minyan

Also by Rabbi Rami M. Shapiro

Wisdom of the Jewish Sages: A Modern Reading of Pirke Avot

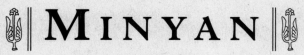

MINYAN

Ten Principles for Living a Life of Integrity

RABBI RAMI M. SHAPIRO

Bell Tower   New York

Published by Bell Tower, an imprint of Harmony Books, a division of Crown Publishers, Inc., 201 East 50th Street, New York, New York 10022. Member of the Crown Publishing Group.

Random House, Inc. New York, Toronto, London, Sydney, Auckland
http://www.randomhouse.com/

Bell Tower and colophon are trademarks of Crown Publishers, Inc.

Printed in the United States of America

Design by Monika Keano/Studio Bird

Library of Congress Cataloging-in-Publication Data is available upon request

ISBN 0-609-80055-8

10 9 8 7 6 5 4 3 2 1

First Edition

To all who,
in the words of Rabbi Abraham Isaac Kook,
dare to make the old new, and to make the new holy

‖ A C K N O W L E D G M E N T S ‖

This book is the culmination of almost two decades of Jewish spiritual teaching, practice, and experimentation within the context of Congregation Beth Or of Miami, Florida. I founded Beth Or with the express purpose of providing myself with a think tank for Jewish mystical and spiritual exploration. I wanted a place where I would be free to learn and share what I learned with others who were hungry for a liberal Torah-based spiritual practice. It grew to become that and much more. Beth Or is my extended family.

The tenfold path of spiritual practice presented here has been tested by members of my congregation, as well as by hundreds of students and religious seekers who have participated in my services, seminars, and workshops over the years. Not all of them found it satisfying or compelling. Yet many did, enough to persuade me to continue my teaching and outreach. It is to them that I owe a great debt of gratitude. Without their love and support I would not have continued to travel the road of a congregational rabbi. Instead I would have privatized my spiritual search and turned inward for meaning and purpose. It would have been a less fulfilling path.

The impetus for this book, however, came not from my practice or my congregation, but from my friend and editor, Toinette Lippe of Bell Tower. It was Toinette who saw in my teaching a "primer for Jewish spirituality." It was she who helped

me shape my practice and ideas for publication. It was she who believed not only in me, but also in my teaching. For that I am eternally grateful. And while I bear sole responsibility for the accuracy and authenticity of the ideas presented here, I owe the clarity of what I write to her.

I owe you, my reader, a debt of thanks as well. There are thousands of books dealing with spiritual teaching and practice. The fact that you would take the time to read mine is humbling, to say the least. I hope you find in these ideas and practices a compass for your own spiritual journey toward awakening.

Rabbi Rami M. Shapiro

CONTENTS

❧ | PREFACE | ❧

The lecture hall was packed. We had come to learn about three of the world's great religions. We were hungry for something new, some spark of insight that would rekindle souls cool with doubt.

The first to speak was a Catholic priest. He sat on a large, straight-backed oak chair with thick rectangular arms and a red velvet seat. He spoke about theology and faith.

The rabbi was next. He sat on a metal folding chair that creaked as he squirmed around on it. He spoke of Jewish history, the Holocaust, *Halacha* (Jewish law), and human rights.

The Buddhist monk was last. He sat on brown cushions placed carefully on a carpet on the floor. He instructed us in meditation: sit up straight, close your eyes, count your breaths one to ten over and again. He invited us to try it, closed his eyes, and said nothing for fifteen minutes. He clapped his hands twice to call us back to attention. "This is Buddhism," he said. "Any questions?"

It has been over twenty-five years since I attended that lecture, and I've never forgotten it. The priest was remote and seemed very sure of himself. He provided us with answers but was not interested in our questions. The rabbi was passionate but abstract. He offered peoplehood to individuals still unsure of selfhood. Only the monk took our seeking seriously. Only he showed us what to *do*. And it was what to do that I wanted to learn.

Certainly Judaism is filled with doing; but the doings to which I was exposed as a child were rituals performed without real purpose or understanding. My family observed the holy days and *Shabbat* (Sabbath) because we were commanded to do so. Fulfilling our obligations to God and tradition seemed to be the whole of Judaism. One was a good Jew if one conformed to the ways of the old Jews. I wanted something more.

Not long after my experience with the Buddhist monk, I attended a lecture by a rabbi who had just published a fiery call for reinvigorating Judaism with kabbalistic insights and practices. He spoke for an hour, outlining the key concepts of Jewish mysticism, and then invited the audience to form a huge circle.

He lighted the braided candle of *Havdalah,* the ceremony separating the Sabbath from the workweek, and asked us to focus on the flame. His voice softened, deepened; he led us into a light trance state. After a few relaxation exercises he guided us through a fantasy world of our own making, helping us find the divine flame within each one of us.

The experience moved me deeply. I was elated to have finally met a teacher of Jewish spirituality. After the talk I managed to get close enough to ask the rabbi: "When can I visit your synagogue and experience more fully what you teach?"

Without missing a beat, he laughed and said: "My synagogue? We don't do this in my synagogue. To tell you the truth, I don't know of any synagogue where you can practice Judaism this way."

I was crushed, saddened, and not a little angry. I felt like

challenging the rabbi to preach what he had just practiced, but the crowd had pressed in on him and I was pushed to the back.

I wanted a Jewish spiritual practice that would infuse my days with light, with joy, with peace, with a transcendent sense of meaning and purpose. I suspected that such a Judaism existed, but I had no idea where to find it. So hungry was I for this spiritual Judaism that I vowed that if I had to, I would create it myself. The *chutzpah* of a nineteen-year-old.

I was fairly new to spirituality, having started my study of world religions two years earlier while still in high school. I had the good fortune to learn from two history teachers, Michael Gelinas and Peter Santos, who had just returned from a summer study program in India. Their enthusiasm was catching. I read every book on Eastern philosophy I could find. I enrolled in a one-day introduction to Zen Buddhism taught by Roshi Philip Kapleau and learned to sit zazen, the meditation practice of the Zen Buddhists. I dreamt hungrily about enlightenment.

My parents worried. Their average Jewish teenager was turning into a "Zen," as they and their friends called it. They feared for my Jewish soul.

In college I majored in philosophy and religion. I continued to meditate daily. I felt myself being drawn deeper and deeper into Zen teaching and practice. I also felt a great deal of guilt about abandoning my Judaism. I had done nothing overt in this regard, but my heart wasn't in the ritual. I knew my parents were concerned, and I wanted to calm their fears. I offered to study in Israel for a year. I went to Israel in search of Zen Judaism and discovered it in the teachings of the Hasidic sages who shaped Jewish life and thought in eighteenth-century Eastern Europe.

Hasidism, from the word *hasid,* or "pious one," was a revolutionary movement among Jews hungry for something more powerful than the dry erudition of the Talmudic scholars that dominated Jewish life in Eastern Europe. The founder of Hasidism, Rabbi Israel ben Eliezer (1700–1760), was called the Baal Shem Tov, a name denoting great skill as a spiritual leader. A *baal shem,* or master of the Name (of God), was an itinerant healer and sage. The Baal Shem Tov (the Good Master of the Name) was the preeminent baal shem.

Unlike most of the great spiritual leaders of Judaism, the Baal Shem Tov at first did not stand out as a Bible scholar or Talmudist. He was not known for his legal acumen or religious asceticism. On the contrary, the stories about the Baal Shem's youth portray him as a simple soul of low social status, who worked as an assistant in a Jewish elementary school. Once married, he dug clay and lime for his wife to sell in the villages of the Carpathian Mountains. Eventually he and his wife ran an inn for wayfarers.

Yet it isn't the outer life of Rabbi Israel that interests Hasidim, but his inner life. For years the Baal Shem Tov would spend hours each day in isolation deep in the forest. There, in communion with God, he evolved his message and teaching style. In 1736 he revealed himself as a healer and a new voice of Judaism.

In 1740 he and his wife moved to Meziboz, a town along

the Polish and Ukrainian border. Students came to listen to the lessons of this new teacher and found a unique message and a teaching style to match. Where the rabbis spoke of law, the Baal Shem spoke of joy. Where the rabbis honed the fine points of Talmud, the Baal Shem told stories about real people in real-life situations struggling to maintain a personal relationship with God.

"God desires the heart," the Baal Shem would remind listeners again and again, quoting from the Talmud;[1] God desires the purity of spirit that all can bring and not the learned mastery with which only some are gifted.

For the Baal Shem Tov "the whole world is full of God's glory,"[2] there is no place and no thing devoid of godliness. Therefore it is unnecessary for Jews to isolate themselves from the pleasures of the world in pursuit of an ascetic and disembodied ideal. On the contrary, true worship is a joyful embracing of the world. When you see something of great beauty, the Baal Shem Tov taught, reflect on the One who fashioned it and in that way allow all life to return you to its Source, the one God.

The Baal Shem Tov died in 1760, entrusting his fledgling movement to Rabbi Dov Baer of Mezerich, who proved to be a great innovator, teacher, and organizer. Hasidism grew and rivaled conventional Judaism for the soul of the European Jew.

In time, however, the movement stagnated. Its emphasis shifted from the spiritual lives of simple Jews to the mystical feats of the *tzaddikim,* the grand masters of competing Hasidic courts. With the rise of *Haskalah,* Jewish rationalism, in the late eighteenth and early nineteenth centuries, Hasidism began to merge with Orthodox Judaism to form a united front against secularism. Hasidic schools adopted a more mainstream Talmudic focus, and Orthodox rabbis decided their differences with Hasidism to be less important than the threat from reason and science. Today Hasidism is seen not as the revolutionary movement it once was, but rather as the extreme right wing of Orthodox Judaism. Few who catch a glimpse of these pious Jews still wearing the clothing of their Eastern European homelands recall the spiritual creativity that was once the heart and soul of their movement.

With the merger of Hasidism into the larger world of Orthodoxy, and the eventual victory of rational thought over mystical revelry, Judaism experienced a steady decline in mystical fervor. The God-filled world celebrated by the Hasidim faded from the general Jewish consciousness, and with it the practices that made that world an everyday reality. What I have done in this book is to reclaim that worldview and recast some of those practices for contemporary liberal Jews.

In 1981 I completed my rabbinic training at the Hebrew Union College–Jewish Institute of Religion and founded Congregation Beth Or in Miami, Florida. My goal was to create a center for a nondenominational, post-Halachic Judaism that used tradition and Hasidic teaching as vehicles for deepening spiritual awareness. The core of Beth Or would be an evolving spiritual philosophy that drew from what I felt was the best of Jewish mystical teaching understood through the lens of contemporary interreligious dialogue, transpersonal psychology, and my own

passion for a nondual understanding of woman, man, and nature as expressions of God.

During my first ten years as rabbi of Beth Or, I developed my philosophy, wrote new liturgies, and experimented with Jewish mystical practice. I shared everything with my congregation. We studied together, *davened* (prayed) together, and struggled to uncover a practical Jewish spirituality that would work for a congregation of middle-class Jewish householders. It took another eight years for this work to come to fruition, emerging as the program I call Minyan.

Minyan is a path of daily spiritual living based on ten *hanhagot,* spiritual disciplines, which have been practiced by Jews for centuries. Minyan is not a substitute for Jewish tradition. You practice Minyan in addition to everything else you do as a Jew. Minyan enriches your Judaism by reclaiming the mystical element that used to be the foundation of tradition.

Minyan has one aim: to awaken you to God as the Source and Substance of Reality. I have practiced Minyan for many years. I have shared these teachings with hundreds of people, both Jew and Gentile, and have found that for those willing to follow them, these ten practices can be powerful vehicles for spiritual living. I hope you will find this true for yourself as well.

‖ MINYAN ‖

INTRODUCTION

My philosophy of Judaism is rooted in a nondual worldview rarely associated with conventional Jewish thought. Mainstream Judaism offers a dualistic understanding of reality that separates God and creation. Nondual Judaism holds that there is no real separation between God and creation. On the contrary, creation is a manifestation of God, the one true Source and Substance of all things. The goal of dualistic Judaism is to bridge the gap between God and humankind. The goal of nondual Judaism is to bring you to the realization that there is no gap.

My understanding of nondual Judaism comes from my study of Jewish mysticism, especially Hasidism. I pull from these sources to articulate a contemporary Jewish spiritual practice I call Minyan.

The word *minyan* refers to the ten Jews needed to form a complete prayer community. I chose the word as a mnemonic for recalling the ten practices I teach. I could have chosen more than ten practices, though I would have been hard-pressed to settle on fewer than ten. I decided on ten because the number ten represents a sense of completeness, and Minyan is a complete system of spiritual practice.

While each of the ten practices of Minyan is rooted in Judaism's ancient past, some of them—meditation, repeating a sacred phrase, and dream interpretation, to name three—are not often associated with traditional Judaism. This is because the

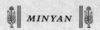

modern Jew's notion of what is traditional Judaism is limited to the ritual aspects of rabbinic Judaism that came to dominate Jewish life in North America and Western Europe over the past century or so. The rich inner life and spiritual practice of Jewish mystics that for centuries informed Judaism receded into the province of Hasidic sects, leaving spiritually searching liberal Jews to turn to other religions for the insights and practices that once were a mainstay of their own tradition. It is part of my mission as a rabbi to reclaim some of these powerful and potentially transformative practices and to present them in a usable form to the contemporary Jewish seeker.

I chose the specific practices of Minyan for one very simple reason—they work. I have experimented with Jewish mystical practice for a long time, and these ten disciplines when practiced together do in fact offer a complete system for personal, interpersonal, and transpersonal growth. They hold out the promise for awakening to God and furthering the creation of a godly world.

I am not a Hasidic Jew. I am a liberal, postdenominational Jew who is drawn to the richness of Hasidic teaching without feeling compelled to follow Hasidic practice. I grew up in an Orthodox environment, but my chosen Jewish lifestyle, while informed by tradition, is not bound by tradition.

I am, however, a Jew in search of God—not as an abstract idea, but as a palpable reality. Many years ago, while still a rabbinic student at the Hebrew Union College–Jewish Institute of Religion in Cincinnati, Ohio, I delivered a sermon on the necessary unity of God, woman, man, and nature. Immediately after the service I was called into the office of the chairman of the philosophy department for a scholarly reprimand.

Referring to my position that God and creation are one, the chairman said: "You, sir, are a megalomaniac."

"With all due respect, Rabbi," I said, "you are wrong. If I understand the term correctly, a megalomaniac thinks he is God. I, on the other hand, know I am God."

What I meant to convey, and doubt very much that I did, was my deep conviction that God is not something or someone living somewhere in or out of time and space. To me God is the One who manifests as all things in time and space. God is not something you pray to, but rather the greater reality to which you awake. For over twenty years, first as a student, then as a rabbi, this nondual understanding of God and creation, and how to awake to it, has defined my spiritual teaching.

I first encountered the nonduality of God at the age of sixteen. I was spending part of the summer of 1967 at a friend's home on Cape Cod, Massachusetts. My friend worked in the local post office every morning, and this provided me with the privacy I needed to continue my meditation practice. I had been sitting zazen (Zen meditation) for several months and found a shady spot near a small lake for a perfect early-morning zendo (Zen meditation center).

I walked there each morning at sunrise, folded several beach towels to make a cushion, and sat cross-legged on the sand. I then attempted to count my breaths, one to ten and over again. Most mornings alternated between counting my breaths and daydreaming. Nothing special happened, but I kept at it nonetheless.

One morning everything changed. At some point my conscious mind stopped counting without replacing that activity with any other. For a moment I was no longer aware of myself sitting on the lakeshore. Everything—the shore, the lake, myself—was gone. There was nothing; not even an awareness of nothing. When the moment passed I was sweating heavily and laughing deeply. Something seemed extremely funny, but I could not tell what it was. Everything was bright; colors appeared more vivid; whatever I looked at seemed to pulsate with a life force I had not noticed before. Without any mental discourse on my part I simply knew that everything was a manifestation of One Thing, and that One Thing was no "thing" at all. The books I was reading at the time called it Reality, Tao, Nature, Universe. I called it God. I still do.

In a sense my whole adult life has been dedicated to renewing that insight for myself and sharing the means of experiencing it with others. This is the single point my rabbinate aims to teach: God is the Source and Substance of all reality, and God is experientially knowable. I do not believe in God as an abstract idea, I experience God as a palpable reality. I know this sounds strange coming from a rabbi. Yet it is not unique to me. Rabbi Yitzhak Epstein of Homel (1780–1857) wrote to a Jewish friend who questioned the authenticity of this nondual understanding of God:

Listen, please, my beloved friend! Do not say that what I am about to say is, God forbid, heresy or philosophy. . . . After doing all the goodly meditations while reciting the songs of praise and the *Shema*[1] . . . it is sensed that, as we say in Yiddish, *Altz is Gott,* All is God.[2]

I believe Reb Yitzhak is right. And I created Minyan to help you discover the truth of this teaching for yourself.

All is God. There is no thing or feeling or thought that is not God, even the idea that there is no God! For this is what it is to be All: God must embrace even God's own negation.

Some people argue that God is a divine spark inside each being. Others claim that God is above and outside creation. I teach neither position. God is not inside or outside, God is the very thing itself! And when there is no thing, but only empty space? God is that as well.

Picture a soup bowl in your mind. Define the bowl. Is it just the material that forms its walls? Or is it the empty space that fills with soup? Without the space the bowl is useless. Without the walls the bowl is useless. So which is the bowl? The answer is both. To be a bowl it must have both being (walls) and emptiness (space).

It is the same with God. For God to be God, for God to be All, God must manifest as both Being and Emptiness. In Judaism we speak of Being and Emptiness as *Yesh* and *Ayin,* respectively.

Yesh (Being) is that manifestation of God that appears to us as separate entities—physical, psychological, and spiritual. Ayin (Emptiness) is that manifestation of God that reveals all separation to be illusory: everything is simply God in differing forms. This teaching is called *shlemut,* the completeness of God. To be complete God must contain all possibilities and paradox.

To be complete God must transcend the notion of opposites and reveal everything as complementary.

God is both Yesh and Ayin, Being and Emptiness, simultaneously. Yesh and Ayin both reside in and are expressions of God's completeness. A confusion often arises when thinking about Yesh and Ayin. People imagine that Yesh is the body and Ayin the soul. Do not equate Yesh with the physical and Ayin with the spiritual. And be careful not to mistake Ayin for God.

Yesh is the world of separateness. Whether you are speaking of bodies or souls, if you imagine them as separate independent beings, you are speaking in terms of Yesh. Ayin is that which is empty of self and separateness. From the perspective of Ayin, there is no separate self, only the oneness of God.

God is not only this oneness, however. God's One is at root two; God's unity necessitates duality. God is both Yesh and Ayin and that which transcends Yesh and Ayin in a Greater Wholeness. It is not that God changes; God does not change. It is your perception of God that changes. When you look at the world as comprising separate entities, you see God as Yesh. When you look at the world as a seamless unity, you see God as Ayin. Both are parts of God, and neither is the whole of God. God cannot be reduced to Yesh or Ayin or even the combination of the two. God is that which embraces both Being and Emptiness in an even greater unity.

In sixteenth-century Safed, Rabbi Moshe Cordovero (1522–1570), one of the most famous and influential teachers of

Zohar, the central text of medieval Jewish mystical thought, explained the greater unity of God this way:

> [God] is found in all things and all things are found in God, and there is nothing devoid of divinity, heaven forfend. Everything is in God, and God is in everything and beyond everything, and there is nothing beside God.[1]

Two centuries later this idea became the foundation of Hasidic Judaism. Rabbi Schneur Zalman of Ladi (1745–1812), the founder of the *Chabad* school of Hasidism, articulated the message thus:

> Everything is God, blessed be He, who makes everything be, and in truth the world of seemingly separate entities is entirely annulled.[2]

Chabad is an acronym comprising the first letters of the Hebrew words *Chochmah*/Wisdom, *Binah*/Understanding, and *Daat*/Knowledge. Chabad emphasizes the capacity of the individual human soul to attain communion with God and places great emphasis on both study and meditation as the central means for doing so. The key to spiritual awakening in Chabad is the temporary annihilation of your sense of separateness. For an instant "you" are gone. In your place there is only a knowing of unity that does not separate knower from the known. There are no words that adequately describe this contentless knowing, yet it is no less real for its indescribability.

Rabbi Aharon haLevi Horowitz of Straosselje (1766–1829) became a disciple of Rabbi Zalman at the age of seventeen. He studied with the rebbe for thirty years and was considered, along with Rabbi Zalman's son, Rabbi Dov Baer, to be one of the two leading lights of Chabad Hasidism. True to his master's teaching, Rabbi Aharon also taught that "there exists in the world no entity other than God, for there is no true substance other than God."[3]

Rabbi Levi Yitzchak of Berdichev (1740–1810) was another noted celebrant of God's unity. Known as the *Darbarimdiger* (the Merciful One), Levi Yitzchak was famous for his compassion and his willingness to give everyone the benefit of the doubt. Unlike his contemporaries in Chabad Hasidism, Levi Yitzchak focused on emotion over reason. For him prayer was an ecstatic encounter with God, and he was known to shake violently during prayer, vibrating from one corner of a room to another, as his soul was caught up in the omnipresence of God. Levi Yitzchak celebrated the nonduality of God in his poem "Dudele":

> Where can I find You—and where can I not find You?
> Above—only You;
> Below—only You;
> To the East—only You;
> To the West—only You;

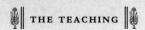

To the South—only You;
To the North—only You;
If it is good—it is You;
If it is not—also You;
It is You; It is only You.

The nondual understanding of reality continued to be the foundation of Jewish mystical teaching right up to our own day. Rabbi Menachem Mendel Schneerson (1902–1994), the seventh Chabad rebbe, taught:

> The absolute reality of God, while extending beyond the conceptual borders of "existence," also fills the entire expanse of existence as we know it. There is no space possible for any other existences or realities we may identify—the objects in our physical universe, the metaphysical truths we contemplate, our very selves . . . do not exist in their own reality; they exist only as an extension of divine energy. . . .[4]

When I seek to share with others this idea of Yesh and Ayin as dual aspects of the nondual God, I often make use of a bar magnet. A magnet has two poles, one positive and one negative. A magnet cannot be otherwise and still be a magnet. The two poles go together, and only when they are together can there be a magnet. Even if you cut the magnet in half and then in half again, it will always manifest these two poles. No matter how small you slice the magnet, its oneness necessitates the duality of positive and negative poles.

Now think of God. Yesh (Being) and Ayin (Emptiness) are the poles of God. God cannot be God without them, and they cannot be themselves without each other and God. This is what is meant by God's shlemut, God's completeness. All things are contained in and necessitated by God. Everything you encounter is a unique manifestation of God. Nothing you encounter is ultimately separate from God. Seeing both Being and Emptiness as expressions of God is called *d'vekut,* God-consciousness. Attaining d'vekut is the aim of the Minyan program.

NECESSARY UNITY

The idea that God and creation are linked in a greater unity is troubling to many. Without a clear distinction between the two, there is often a fear that individuality will be devalued and nature diminished. The implication of nonduality, however, is just the opposite.

The essence of reality is an all-encompassing Unity that embraces and indeed generates relative diversity. It is not that you and I are creatures fashioned by God. It is rather that you and I are temporary manifestations of God. We are real. We are worthwhile. We are unique. What we are not is eternal, separate, and independent. We are God, though certainly not the totality of God.

The relationship between God and creation is like that between an ocean and its waves. Each wave, while unique and distinct in time and space, is a manifestation of the same ocean. Without the ocean there could be no wave. Yet waves are no less real for their having no existence separate from the ocean. Waves are no less distinct one from the other for their each being manifestations of the same ocean.

Similarly, you and I, and the myriad details of creation, are no less real for being manifestations of the one God. Our separate reality is dependent upon that larger unity. Our separate reality is momentary, transient, and relative, but that does not make it illusory or unreal.

The aim of Jewish spiritual practice is to become conscious of both the wave and the ocean, the relative and the absolute. The Jewish mystic celebrates the self even as she experiences its transience. She honors the other even as she recognizes it as part of herself and the Greater Unity from which both arise. Jewish spirituality is not an "either/or" proposition; it is profoundly and unrelentingly "and."

Jewish spiritual practice does not supplant the self with the One, but awakens the self to its inseparability from the One. Jewish spiritual practice awakens you to the complementary awareness of the One and the Many as equal manifestations of God and allows you to function in the relative world of separate selves, while at the same time encountering through that relative world the absolute world of inseparable unity. It is not that the relative is more or less real than the absolute, but that both are authentic expressions of God, as we encounter God.

Rabbi Aharon haLevi Horowitz, Schneur Zalman's great disciple, taught this idea centuries ago.

God's only desire is to reveal unity through diversity. That is, to reveal that all of reality is unique in all of its levels and in all of its details, and nevertheless united in a fundamental oneness.[1] The main point of creation . . . [is] to reveal the wholeness of God from the opposite perspective. . . . For it is the nature of completeness to include all opposites in the One.[2]

Rabbi Aharon's point is crucial to understanding Jewish spiritual practice. The goal is not to exchange one opposite for another, but to see that all opposites are manifestations of God, the one true Reality. Heaven is no more divine than earth. An angel is no more holy than your neighbor. A rock is no less a manifestation of God than a rabbit. There is a profound equivalence among the animate and the inanimate, and at the same time there is a profound difference.

You must hold both the relative and the absolute in mind simultaneously, seeing them both as manifestations of the greater nondual reality of God. This is the essence of Jewish spiritual practice. It cannot be done by retreating into one half of the whole or the other. It can be done only by allowing each half to take its place in the whole.

The thirteenth–century Spanish kabbalist Abraham Abulafia speaks of this in terms of pouring a jug of water into a flowing stream. The water from the jug is no less present in the stream, but neither is it separate from the stream. Through sustained spiritual practice you can pour your ego into the stream of God and fulfill your humanity by realizing your divinity.

> For now he [the awakened individual] is no longer separated from God, and behold he is God and God is he; for he is so intimately adhering to God that he cannot by any means be separate from God, for he is God. See now that I, even I, am God. He is I and I am He.[3]

This is the voice of spiritual awakening: He is I and I am He! It is an ecstatic overcoming of ego-centered consciousness by a greater boundaryless awareness. It is not so much that the ego is gone for good, but that it is no longer in opposition to anything. The self defines itself no longer in terms of the other, but as a manifestation of the whole.

Being a manifestation of the whole obligates you to the whole. Knowing that you are not separate from the rest of creation awakens you to the fact that you are responsible to creation. Too often people imagine that being empty of separate selfhood means that nothing matters; the world is a game, an illusion, a worthless place from which the soul seeks to escape. This is not the Jewish view.

The fact that you are a temporary manifestation of God does not mean you are unimportant. On the contrary, you are a unique and unreproducible expression of the Divine that is endowed with irreducible value and holiness. You are a vehicle of godliness placed here to bring godliness to bear on every aspect of life as you encounter it. And that means recognizing and honoring the godliness of all other things.

There is a mistaken understanding among many that spirituality is in opposition to this-worldly concerns. Many who cling to spiritual practice do so in order to transcend this world, to escape the ordinary, and to find refuge in the extraordinary. Within Judaism there is no dichotomy between everyday life and holiness. Your charge is to be holy and to make the world holy. Your spiritual practice reveals your interconnectedness with the world and the interconnectedness of the world with God. No longer deluded into seeing yourself in opposition to others, you cannot separate yourself or your actions from the impact they have on others. The awakening of unity is accompanied by a powerful sense of shared suffering, compassion, and a compelling need to do justly in the world. There is no escaping the world, but a deep and compassionate embracing of it. You are challenged to uplift the world with justice and compassion, not to transcend it with mystical revelry.

Judaism, perhaps far more than any of the world's major religions, is a religion for householders. It is not something you do instead of marrying, raising a family, managing a career, and paying bills. Judaism is the way you do all these things. This is what Torah means when she challenges you to be holy. You are asked to manifest holiness in the ordinary events of your everyday life. Make eating holy. Make conversation holy. Make sleeping holy. Make sex holy.

Making life holy requires you to see all things as manifestations of God, the Source and Substance of all that was, is, and will be. Making life holy obligates you to live your life and help others live theirs according to the highest ethical and moral standards. You do not meditate in order to see beyond the suffering of your neighbor. You meditate in order to see the suffering of your neighbor as clearly as you see your own. You do not practice Judaism to escape the pain of ordinary living. You practice Judaism to alleviate that pain for both yourself and the world. But you cannot do this if you continue to see your neighbor as other than yourself.

Awakening to the unity of self and other in the Greater Unity of God kindles your deepest sense of compassion and empowers you to repair the world with justice. Jewish spirituality is not about escaping from the world, but about recognizing, honoring, and caring for even its smallest part.

When I teach this spiritual ideal to children I often use a midsize jigsaw puzzle depicting the earth floating in the deep black of space. I pour the pieces onto a table and ask the children to put the puzzle together. What they don't know is that I have removed one piece and put it in my pocket. It is a small piece of blue-black space, one among dozens of the same color.

After a while the puzzle is complete, all but the missing piece. I ask the children how they feel about the puzzle. They are frustrated: all that work and they can't finish.

"But it is such a small piece," I remind them. "There are so many just like it. You can certainly see what the whole puzzle looks like without that missing piece."

"Yes, but it isn't done. It has a hole in it."

"But it is such a small hole. One missing piece among hundreds that are here. Can it really matter that much?"

"Yes!" they cry, upset at my seeming lack of understanding. "Without that piece nothing is right. It just isn't right!"

Then I take the piece out of my pocket and wait for the groans to subside.

"Look at this piece. It is so small. So simple. And not so different from the others. In fact, when we place this piece in the puzzle it will be hard to tell exactly where it is; it will blend in so

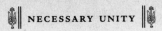

evenly. And yet how you missed it! How important it was to you! How central to your completion of the puzzle!

"Now listen very carefully: Each of us is just like this piece. We are not so different from all the other pieces of the universe; looked at from outer space, we just blend in. And yet, just like this piece, we are absolutely essential to the whole.

"If we care so much about this little piece of the puzzle, how much more must we care about ourselves and each other."

WHO ARE YOU?

Torah teaches that you are created in the image of God, the One beyond Yesh and Ayin, Being and Emptiness, that is the Source and Substance of them both.[1] From the Jewish mystical perspective, being created in the image of God means that you are God manifest in a particular time and place. Being a manifestation of God, you, too, must contain both Yesh and Ayin. And so you do.

In human beings Yesh and Ayin appear as two distinct modes of consciousness: *Yetzer ha-Rah* and *Yetzer ha-Tov,* the human inclinations for doing evil and for doing good, respectively.

Yetzer ha-Rah is your capacity to perceive uniqueness, differences, otherness. It is your ability to focus on yourself alone and to separate yourself from everything else. Your Yetzer ha-Rah sees every living thing as an entity unto itself, as unique and apart from the whole. Why call it *rah,* evil? Because without the balancing insight of the Yetzer ha-Tov, the inclination for unity, the Yetzer ha-Rah's insistence on separate self and independence pits one life against another, destroying any hope for community, justice, and compassion.

Yet a world without Yetzer ha-Rah is no less evil. Yetzer ha-Tov is your capacity to perceive the interdependence of things, your inclination to bridge differences, to build community, to effect harmony. Without the balancing vision of Yetzer ha-Rah, however, it is also the capacity to overlook diversity, to ignore uniqueness, to work toward a homogeneity that can be quite dull, threatening, and ultimately lifeless. Without the ability to recognize and respect individual differences, justice is reduced to totalitarianism, compassion to pity, and community to conformity.

A healthy world needs both Yetzer ha-Rah, with its welcoming of and respect for individuality, and Yetzer ha-Tov, with its insight into interdependence and harmony. The human mind contains both inclinations and must use each to balance the other. In this way the mind becomes whole. When the mind is whole the human becomes holy.

As long as you live under the dictates of the Yetzer ha-Rah, the illusion of separateness and independence, you will forever seek to control what happens to you. You will strive to hold on to pleasantness and avoid pain. You will go to great lengths to fulfill your desires, and when you are frustrated in your efforts (which must happen since you are not in control of what life brings) you will become angry or depressed or both.

As long as you identify one-sidedly with Yetzer ha-Rah, you will be unbalanced, selfish, isolated, anxious, and prone to all sorts of physical and mental diseases. The cure is to balance your perspective by tapping the Yetzer ha-Tov.

There is nothing wrong with the Yetzer ha-Rah's sense of self as long as you realize that self is temporary, changing, and without independent existence, all of which is taught by the Yetzer ha-Tov. Only a self that knows its own transience is healthy, for only such a self can honor both Yetzer ha-Rah and Yetzer ha-Tov.

Yet if you were to identify too strongly with the Yetzer ha-

Tov, you would seek to impose the absolute oneness of Ayin on the relative diversity of Yesh. You would insist upon a homogeneity among the things of this world and eliminate free will and choice. Justice and compassion would be of no concern to you, for you would see everything as the unfolding of fate. You would no longer see the other as an other, respecting differences and acknowledging boundaries. Everything would be seen as an extension of yourself, though you would not recognize this megalomania, but rather assume that your view must be God's as well.

There is nothing wrong with the Yetzer ha-Tov's sense of oneness as long as you realize that oneness is only half the story; that diversity, too, is a part of God's completeness. The healthy self must know its value and its limitations. It must honor itself as a self and others as separate selves through the conscience and balanced use of Yetzer ha-Rah. And it must recognize its fundamental emptiness of permanence and its interconnectedness with all life and God through the conscientious and balanced cultivation of Yetzer ha-Tov.

Among the many texts that articulate this truth, I find this poem by Reb Nachum of Chernobyl to be the most striking:

If I am I and you are you,
then
I am I and you are you.
But if I am I because you are you,
then
I am not I and you are not you.

The Yetzer ha-Rah sees the I as I and the you as you: separate, distinct, independent. As long as this is the dominant outlook, you and I are in conflict. The Yetzer ha-Tov sees you and me as interdependent; we arise together and make no sense without each other. When this becomes the dominant outlook, the I is no less I, but, on the contrary, far more than I; it is you as well. And the you is no less you: on the contrary, it is more; it is I as well.

It is the aim of spiritual practice to balance your two inclinations and in this way channel your capacity through self to unity. Nothing is lost or rejected; rather, everything is integrated and lifted up. The next time you ask yourself, "Why am I here? Why was I born?" think of this: You are here to unify the Yetzer ha-Rah and the Yetzer ha-Tov in yourself in order to recognize the greater unity of Yesh and Ayin in God.

From the perspective of Yesh the world is a collection of diverse, separate, and transient beings competing with one another for survival. From the perspective of Ayin, the world is a homogeneous oneness without time, space, and separate beings. To become attached to either perspective is to miss the greater completeness of God.

God as God, however, cannot "know" this completeness, for "knowing" requires that one is separate from that which is known, and nothing is separate from God. Yet the completeness of God requires that knowing. Thus it is inherent in the very nature of God to manifest a being capable of perceiving both relative and absolute and that which includes both—that is, the Greater Unity of God. The human being is that being.

You are created to know the Greater Unity of God. You are not here to amass fortunes. You are not here to win wars or competitions. You are not here to earn rewards or make for yourself a great name. You are here to know God. You are not an accident. You are a necessary extension of God's Greater Wholeness.

It is this Greater Wholeness that lies at the heart of all spiritual awakening. The question is: How do we awaken to it? There are many fine and powerful answers. The one I offer here, the one that defines my rabbinate and my daily life, is called Minyan, a tenfold path of Jewish spiritual practice.

THE TEN VOWS

Minyan is not something you should take up lightly. It is a program of serious spiritual discipline that requires true commitment. For this reason, I ask people who desire to practice Minyan to take ten vows based on the Ten Commandments to help promote the depth of commitment needed to practice Minyan. I have reworked the Ten Commandments into vows, adapting them to a highly personal and direct style I learned from Vietnamese Zen master Thich Nhat Hanh, whose reading of Buddhism opened my eyes to the power of the Ten Commandments as daily affirmations of spiritual intent.

There is a real difference between a commandment and a vow, especially as Buddhists understand the latter term. A commandment is an order levied upon one by a superior. A vow is a personal statement of intent. The former implies an enforceable hierarchy of power; the latter relies solely on your own integrity. One who breaks a commandment is liable for punishment. One who fails to keep a vow is liable to self-incrimination. One can and should return to a vow over and over again to bolster one's intention to proceed with the avowed action. It is a matter not of breaking a rule and being punished, but of recognizing one's limits and recommitting to a goal.

I chose this approach to the Ten Commandments for several reasons. First, the term "Ten Commandments" is not found in the Torah. Judaism refers to the *Aseret ha-Debrot,* the Ten

Sayings or Ten Utterances, spoken by God at Mount Sinai. While the Torah is clear that it is God who sets these ideals in place, they are spoken in the context of principles, not laws. I wanted to move away from the legal aspect of commandment and focus more on the principled nature of these teachings.

Second, the common understanding of the Hebrew word *mitzvah,* commandment, as meritorious obligation or good deed misses the deeper meanings of the word. While classical Judaism takes *mitzvot* (the plural of mitzvah) to be divinely revealed commands levied on the people by a divine king, my teacher Rabbi Arthur Waskow speaks of a mitzvah as an act that connects the actor with the larger world and with God. Rabbi Waskow translates the traditional blessing spoken before performing a mitzvah ("Blessed are You, King of the Universe who sanctifies us with His Commandments and Who commands us to . . .") as "Blessed is the One Who makes us holy by connecting us with holiness, and teaches us to connect through the practice of . . ."

Third, fewer and fewer liberal Jews relate to the concept of divinely revealed commandments. Instead they take mitzvot to refer to customs, good deeds, or folkways that may sustain Jewish culture but no longer speak to their original aim of connecting the doer with God. Since it is our connection to God, our awakening to the relative and the absolute within the greater wholeness of the divine, our personal and collective encounter with Levi Yitzchak's omnipresent You, that is my sole concern, I did not want to confuse the issue by using words that are commonly misconstrued.

Many Minyan practitioners repeat these ten vows each morning upon arising. Others use them as part of their Shabbat evening practice, reading them after lighting the Shabbat candles. Still others have made posters of the vows and taped them up on walls as reminders. However you choose to use these vows, the goal is to begin your study of Minyan with the commitment spiritual practice deserves.

Read these ten vows carefully. First seek only to understand their meaning and intent. Then ask yourself whether or not they speak to you. Do they challenge you to live up to the principles they espouse? If they do, read them aloud as an affirmation of intent. Speak them as an act of ownership and commitment: This is what I am about as a religious person. These are among the core ideals I seek to manifest in my life through my actions. These are the pillars of truth I lean upon in my quest for spiritual awakening.

1

YHVH,

the Unnamed and Unnameable Reality, is God, the Source and Substance of all Being and Becoming.

Aware that the ego forever creates gods in its own image for its own profit, I vow to recognize all ideas about God as products of human culture, bound by history and circumstance, and forever incapable of defining and describing the Reality Beyond Naming.

Aware that the human being is capable of encountering

God and of articulating that encounter through myth, metaphor, art, and music, I vow to enter into dialogue with other faiths and their followers to appreciate and experience more fully the depth of human spirituality, insight, and creativity. In this way do I vow to establish a common bond with all spiritual seekers, recognizing that we are each particularist practitioners of a Universal Truth.

2

YHVH
cannot be imagined and must not be imaged.

Aware of the suffering caused by allegiance to dogma and creed, I vow never to make idols of ideas or to mistake any *ism* for the *Is*.

All religious teaching is human in origin and therefore subject to error, illusion, prejudice, pride, and politics. All religions are false insofar as they claim to be true. All religions are true insofar as they recognize and admit to being false. I vow to practice meditation as a means of emptying the mind of thought and image and thereby awakening to God.

3

**Do not misuse religion or spirituality by taking God
in vain.**

Aware of the suffering caused by the misuse of God and religion in the quest of power, I vow never to mistake my path as the Path, my truth as the Truth, my idea of God as God, YHVH, Reality, but

to surrender my opinion to the greater unknowing that is the
One Beyond Knowing.

I dedicate myself to humility in matters of the spirit, recognizing that at best I glimpse but an infinitesimal slice of the infinite Whole.

4
Remember the Sabbath and set it apart.

Aware of the suffering caused by unmindful living, I vow to cultivate Shabbat as a weekly day of mindfulness and attention, setting it aside for rest, renewal, reflection, and re-creation.

I vow to cultivate the Sabbaths of the seventh year and
the seventh cycle of years.

In the sabbatical year I vow to rethink my priorities and
reassess the decisions I have made that have brought me to this
place in my life. I vow to make the changes that may be necessary
to set my life firmly on a just and compassionate path.

In the jubilee year I vow to free myself of debt and to help
free those who are indebted to me. I vow to work toward a just
world where all are free to develop their fullest potential.

5
Honor your mother and your father.

Aware of the suffering caused by old age, illness, and death, I vow
to care for my parents to the best of my ability.

Recognizing that no parent is perfect, I acknowledge the sacrifices that were made on my behalf and the role my own behavior played and continues to play in my family's evolution.

I vow to cultivate reconciliation with my parents and to merit their respect by living according to the highest that is in me.

I vow to promote the well-being of all elderly people, doing what I can to honor and respect both aging and the aged and seeing in the old a repository of wisdom and experience necessary for right living and a healthy and honorable society.

6

Do not murder.

Aware of the suffering caused by the needless and wanton destruction of life, I vow to cultivate compassion and justice and learn ways to protect the well-being of people, animals, plants, and minerals.

I am determined not to murder, not to let others murder, and not to condone any act of murder in the world, in my thinking, and in my way of life.

I recognize that murder refers not only to the literal taking of life, but to the killing of dignity. I vow to practice gentleness and respect toward all, learning how to struggle for what is right without falling prey to what is wrong.

7

Do not engage in sexual misconduct.

Aware of the suffering caused by sexual misconduct, I vow to cultivate sexual responsibility and not to engage in sexual relations without compassion and commitment.

I am determined to respect my commitments and the commitments of others. I will do everything in my power to protect children and adults from sexual abuse and to eliminate sexually transmitted disease.

I vow to honor my body and the bodies of others by treating all beings with respect and dignity.

I vow to hallow pleasure and the senses by seeing the wonder of life within and around me.

I vow to uphold the holiness of sexuality by never degrading it, myself, or another through violence, ignorance, or deceit.

8

Do not steal.

Aware of the suffering caused by exploitation, social injustice, theft, and oppression, I vow to practice acts of loving-kindness toward all things.

I vow to practice generosity by sharing my time, energy, and material resources with those in need.

I vow not to steal or keep anything that should belong to

others. I will respect the property of others, yet work for the wise use of all earthly resources.

I vow to cultivate peace by refraining from acts of violence (both verbal and physical), doing whatever I can to protect others from violence, and working with others to end violence in society as a whole.

9
Do not lie.

Aware of the suffering caused by wrongful speech and shallow listening, I vow to cultivate compassionate speech and attentive listening.

I vow to speak truthfully, with words that inspire self-confidence, joy, compassion, justice, and hope.

I am determined not to spread news that I do not know to be certain or to share information that will cause needless harm.

I vow not to criticize or condemn things of which I am not sure and to cultivate an open mind.

I will refrain from uttering words that cause needless division or discord, and I will make every effort to reconcile differences peacefully and compassionately and resolve all conflicts, however small.

10
Do not covet.

Aware of the suffering caused by unmindful consumption, I vow to cultivate ethical eating, drinking, and consuming, to promote both personal and planetary well-being.

I vow to live simply, to enjoy what I have before seeking to have more, and to labor for that which I desire honestly and justly.

I vow to honor the differing gifts of people and to respect the property of others, seeing in another's success inspirational lessons for my own efforts.

❧ ‖ THE PRACTICE ‖ ❧

I have taught Minyan seminars and spirituality workshops for almost twenty years, and I am still amazed to hear people speak of spiritual practice as if it were the easiest and safest thing in the world. It is neither.

Among the many Hebrew terms for spiritual practice is *avodah,* work. Spirituality is a discipline. When people say to me, "I'm a spiritual person," they often mean that they treasure some vague feeling of connection with God, nature, and humanity that is most often divorced from any behavioral obligation. Spirituality is not a feeling, nor is it vague. Spirituality is a conscious practice of living out the highest ethical ideals in the concreteness of your everyday life. The disembodied spirituality so often spoken about by those who do not practice any spiritual discipline rarely obligates them to anything and often excuses the grossest behavior.

During one of my seminars a woman said to me: "Rabbi, I don't have any need of these disciplines. I am a holy person by nature." She then went on to explain her superiority to the common man and woman and how much compassion she felt for them. Throughout the weekend seminar she demonstrated the depth of her holiness by making fun of and gossiping about most of the other participants.

Divorcing God from deed violates the very essence of spirituality as a means of manifesting holiness in the ordinary reality of your everyday life. Spirituality is the process whereby you live out the moral and ethical implications of the Greater Unity of Yesh (Being) and Ayin (Emptiness). Recognizing the interconnectedness of self and other, human being and nature, obligates you to act toward others and nature in a manner that is quintessentially just and compassionate.

A participant in one of my weekend retreats asked a very important question: "Can an enlightened person do wrong?" The students quickly fell into two camps. One side argued that it is impossible for an enlightened person to do wrong. While they admitted that from the point of view of an unenlightened person the actions of an enlightened person might appear wrong, in fact they are true to a higher principle that most people cannot grasp. To illustrate this point one woman told us about her spiritual teacher, who chased her through the meditation center in a drunken fury, wielding a carving knife and threatening to kill her. She locked herself in her room until his rage passed. Later, after some reflection, she realized that he meant her no harm. He was trying to help her confront her own mortality. I wonder.

The others argued that enlightened people are still people and subject to the same flaws as the rest of us. They can, and do, make mistakes and do wrong. The Jewish position is clearly with the second group. The Talmud puts it succinctly: "The greater the sage, the greater the evil inclination."

There is nothing mysterious about spiritual practice or the lives of spiritual teachers. They are men and women with the same flaws as all of us. While they may be more knowledgeable in the area of spiritual practice, that in and of itself does not make them immune to misbehavior. Being spiritual does not in any way free you from having to be moral as most of us define moral. We must demand at least the same standard of ethical behavior of our spiritual teachers as we do of our friends. Maybe more.

When the participants asked me for my opinion I said simply: Truly spiritual people can do great evil. Unlike most of us, however, they are acutely aware of this fact. It is this awareness that allows them to choose not to do wrong. It is for them, as it is for us, always a matter of choice.

Whenever you see a spiritual teacher behaving in a manner that is clearly wrong, do not excuse it, but challenge it. If the teacher is truly spiritual, he or she will thank you for your concern. If he or she berates you with claims of a higher morality, find yourself another teacher.

Learning from a loving and compassionate spiritual teacher can be one of the deepest joys of spiritual practice. It can also be one of its greatest dangers.

There is another difficulty in spiritual practice that has nothing to do with the teacher and everything to do with the teaching. Spiritual awakening can challenge your most fundamental and cherished views of yourself and your world. Not everyone can handle it.

In the *Ayin Yaacov,* an anthology of Talmudic legends from the first five centuries of the Common Era, we find this famous tale of mystical ascent that vividly portrays the potential dangers of spiritual practice:

Four sages entered the heavenly garden of spiritual awakening: Ben Azai, Ben Zoma, Elisha ben Abuyya, and Rabbi Akiva. "Ben Azai gazed upon the mystery and died. Ben Zoma gazed and went mad. Ben Abuyya gazed and lost faith. Only Rabbi Akiva entered in peace and departed in peace."[1]

Madness, death, apostasy; why are these so starkly linked to spiritual awakening? Because awakening to God can be dangerous. It requires the abandonment of everything you think you know about the world and your place in it. Regardless of your religious or philosophical commitments, the actual experience of God lifts you out of the known and comfortable.

No matter what your philosophy, you are a human being. No matter how committed you may be to the idea of nonduality, your everyday reality still smacks of duality. You live with the assumption of separate selves. Gazing upon the mystery, awakening to God, strips you of the last vestiges of duality and absorbs you in a boundaryless sea of nonduality. The full realization of nonduality necessitates a temporary loss of self. Only the strongest can endure this without trauma. Look what happened to these sages.

Ben Azai died. In the face of the Infinite the finite is nullified, but only in the absolute sense. The Infinite, to be infinite, must include and make room for the finite. Again, the seeming opposites of absolute and relative, infinite and finite, part and whole, self and other, must be seen in the context of a greater unity that affirms diversity. Nondual reality is not opposed to dualism, but embraces it in a greater unity. Failure to grasp this requires a rejection of one extreme or the other. Reject finity and death is the result. Reject infinity and faith is lost.

Ben Azai found the experience of selflessness so wonderful that he could not leave. He abandoned the relative world of Yesh for the absolute world of Ayin. And in doing so, he had to divest himself of himself. He had to die.

Ben Zoma went mad. His worldview was turned inside out; he was unable to hold on to the relative while experiencing the absolute. Yet this is exactly what is asked of you. Jewish mystical practice is not at the expense of everyday living; it is everyday living. Spiritual awakening does not demand the once and for all dismantling of ego, but rather the placing of ego in the larger context of God.

Ego is not the enemy. Ego has a positive and necessary role to play in the larger scheme of things. Ego may appear to be the enemy when you first glimpse the fact that it has defined the world in its own image. You may imagine you have to kill the ego to save yourself, but you cannot function without ego. Nor can you function optimally with only the ego. You need the ego to run the affairs of your normal waking-state consciousness. But ego must take a backseat when you begin to see the Whole as whole rather than as a loose confederation of competing parts.

Ben Zoma could not put ego in its proper context and thus lost self to madness.

Like the others, Elisha ben Abuyya was caught up in the either/or illusion: life or death; part or whole. And like them, he made a choice, rejecting the infinite by rejecting the teachings and techniques that lead to it.

The wonderfully fascinating thing about Elisha is that his

loss of faith came after a successful test of faith. He did not reject religion because it failed to deliver on its promise. He rejected it precisely because it did deliver. He just did not like what he received. What he wanted was the world he had been promised: a heavenly abode where right is rewarded and evil punished. What he found was nonduality: the interdependence and impermanence of all things arising from and manifest in the impersonal nature of divinity. And he rejected it.

Only Akiva returned unscathed. Why? Because he "entered in peace and departed in peace." *Shalom*, peace, shares a root with *shalem*, wholeness. Akiva entered this state of awakening already whole. True peace is being whole, integrated, your self at one with the universe.

Akiva's "departure" can be understood in two ways. First is the departure of the separate self that comes with the tapping of the nonduality of reality. The ego dies; the self departs. There is a unity of Knower, Knowing, and Known. In this unity there is no room for the differentiations so vital to self and ego. This is the moment of absolute unity without diversity. But this monism of Ayin is no more the whole than its dualistic twin, Yesh.

As Rabbi Menachem Mendel Schneerson, the recently deceased rebbe of Chabad Hasidism, wrote:

> To begin to understand God we must learn to go beyond our own mind, our own ego, our own tools of perception. Only then will God emerge. To look for God with our eyes, with our intellect, with our logic, would be

like trying to capture the sun's light in our hand. God is not definable. . . . We recognize the paradox that God is beyond reality as we know it, while at the same time encompassing reality. That God is able to create both the finite and the infinite, the physical and the transcendent—because He is beyond both. . . .[2]

The universe is both many and one and that which embraces them both. Akiva knew that he was not an isolated self, but part of a greater unity. Thus when he encountered that unity and momentarily lost the sense of separate self, there was no rupture. And when he departed from that monistic state of absolute oneness and again sensed himself as a self, he did so without losing his knowledge of selflessness. Akiva knew that self and selflessness are parts of the greater nonduality of God, and he attached himself to neither.

This was Akiva's genius. His spiritual awakening was not at the expense of his ordinary living. His ordinary living was not at the expense of his spiritual awakening. To one who is whole and at peace, this world is the world-to-come. It is not a matter of exchanging one reality for another, or of leaving a false world for a truer one. It is a matter of recognizing that all is God.

The practices of Minyan that follow are not an attempt to escape from the everyday world. They are the means by which you engage that world more deeply. They are to be integrated into your daily life, and the more regular they become, the more life will reveal the unity of Yesh and Ayin. The deeper you go with

Minyan, the less you define yourself according to Yesh ("I am I because I am I") and the more you awaken to the interdependence of all things as Ayin ("I am I because you are you"). In time you will cling to neither Yesh nor Ayin and recognize both as necessary manifestations of the one true reality, God.

Some of you will take to Minyan, some of you won't. Among those who find it enticing, some of you will stick with it, some of you won't. There is nothing magical here. There is no secret to spiritual practice. It is a choice you make every day: Will you sit in meditation? Will you repeat your sacred phrase? Will you follow the other practices? No one can make these choices for you; and it would be foolish to think that you can choose once and for all.

Every day is a new struggle. The more often you choose to practice, the easier the choice becomes, but it is always a choice. All I can say about the efficacy of Minyan is this: Each of these practices has centuries of history behind it. It has worked for thousands and thousands of people. It works for me. Dedicate yourself to the program for six months and see if it works for you as well.

THE TEN PRACTICES OF MINYAN

Avodah be-Bittul/Meditation

Gerushin/Repetition

Musar/Inspirational Reading

Kavvanah/Attention

Tzedakah/Generosity

Gemilut Chesed/Kindness

Pitron Chalomot/Dream Interpretation

Eco-kashrut/Ethical Consumption

Teshuvah/Self-Perfection

Shabbat/Sabbath

AVODAH BE-BITTUL
Meditation

Meditation is, quite simply, the ending of thought. It is not joy, deep contemplation, wonder, amazement, or even awakening. It is the cessation of thought.

What happens when thoughts cease? I don't know. Without thoughts there is no thinker. Without a thinker there is no knower or thing known. Without these there is no way to answer the question "What happens when thoughts cease?" Meditation is a profound unknowing.

Saying that I do not know what happens when thought stops, however, is not the same as saying that I do not know the benefits of meditation practice, or that I do not know what happens when thoughts are rekindled and the mind leaps back into everyday waking consciousness. When thoughts return and I am once more aware of myself as a separate self, I recognize profound changes. I am less tense and more composed. My thought processes are less rigid and a little more subtle. The world I sense around me seems more alive: colors are more vibrant, sounds are more sweet, the details of things seem to stand out more vividly.

There is a joy that accompanies me when I return from meditative practice. I find myself smiling more easily and broadly. I feel more in sync with my surroundings. These sensations are not the goals of meditation, but its by-products. The "goal" is simply the thing itself; the result of meditation is ending the mind's chatter and putting the self in the larger context of the Whole of which it is a part. And that, of course, is the greatest benefit of meditation practice.

Whenever I introduce meditation to a Jewish audience there is always skepticism: Is meditation really Jewish? Why didn't I learn this in Sunday school? Why doesn't my rabbi teach this?

Yes, meditation is Jewish. Only two centuries ago, during the height of Hasidism's popularity in Eastern Europe, meditation of one sort or another was practiced by thousands of Jews in hundreds of synagogues. It was considered axiomatic that individuals could converse with God and that rabbis could teach them how to do so. Yet the meditative Judaism of the *shtetl* (village) never made it into the mainstream American synagogue. The reason so many Jews are ignorant of the Jewish meditative tradition is that so many rabbis found it incongruent with American life and the American Judaism they sought to perpetuate.

In America religion was concerned more with civic duty and ethical action than with spirituality and encounter with God. Mainstream American Judaism tended to focus on ethics, ritual observance, and Jewish politics. God took a backseat to tradition, and spirituality was replaced with social action. While appealing to the prophetic tradition and its concern with universal justice, the liberal American rabbinate ignored the intense personal connection the prophets felt with God.

Though pockets of Hasidim continued to practice the meditative techniques of the sages, their self-isolating lifestyle removed them and their teaching from contact with the majority of Jews. It wasn't until the 1960s that outreach to Jews by the Chabad Hasidim began to break down some of these barriers.

At that time Jewish youth were discovering a hunger for God and spiritual teaching and practice. Alongside the much more public political upheavals of the 1960s a more quiet revolution was occurring in the souls of many younger Jews. They had been raised on the ideals of the prophets; they had been initiated into the ritual of their people; but they longed for a more soulful encounter with reality. They knew the outer form of goodness, but they longed for the inner transformation of holiness.

The sudden interest in spirituality caught, and in many cases continues to catch, the leaders of American Judaism by surprise. They themselves were barely fluent in spiritual practice. They had not thought it necessary. God had given the Torah to the people, what more did they need? After all, if you read a wonderful book on ethical living, you don't need to call the author, you only need to practice what the book suggests. Rabbis and synagogues were prepared to expound the Book; they just never thought it necessary to provide a link to its Author. So when challenged to teach an experimental approach to God, they balked, and Jewish youth turned elsewhere.

Hindu ashrams and Buddhist meditation halls filled with Jews far beyond their numbers in the general population. So prevalent was the presence of Jews in Eastern religions that Swami Satchidananda once remarked to Rabbi Zalman Schachter-Shalomi: "How spiritual your people are! Wherever I go, whatever temple or ashram I visit, the place is filled with Jews."

Today the situation is changing. Meditation is being rediscovered in Judaism. New books exploring Jewish mysticism and spiritual practice appear almost monthly. Jewish retreat centers advertise spiritual weekends, and rabbis around the United States are beginning to teach the art of Jewish meditation. Minyan is part of this rediscovery and renewal, drawing upon a meditative tradition within Judaism that goes back thousands of years.

Moses Maimonides (1135–1204), the great medieval physician and philosopher, saw meditation as central to the lives of the biblical prophets. The prophets neither willed their prophecies nor waited passively for God to bestow them. Instead, Maimonides believed, they engaged in meditative practices designed to attune their minds to prophecy. They made themselves ready to receive the ethical teachings of God.[1]

The prophets were not the only Jews to develop and practice formal meditation. The Talmud tells us that the early rabbis would "be still one hour prior to each of the three prayer services, then pray for one hour, and afterwards be still again for one hour more."[2] The technique used by these rabbis was not preserved, although Maimonides interprets the notion of being still to refer to maintaining a motionless posture "in order to settle their minds and quiet their thoughts."[3]

The rabbis also formulated the eighteen benedictions of the *Amidah* (Standing) as a meditative practice. The Amidah is the central prayer of each of the three daily worship services established by the rabbis. The Talmud tells us that its original function was as a silent chant designed to bring the worshipper into the presence of God. The Talmud goes on to say that the great sages would spend an hour reciting the Amidah alone.

The Amidah is to be recited without interruption, with each benediction flowing directly into the next. The recitation is accompanied by ritual bowing. When reciting the word *baruch* (blessed), one should bend the knees. When saying the next word, *ata* (are You), one should bow from the waist. This bowing takes place at the beginning and end of the first and next-to-last paragraphs of the Amidah. The Talmud suggests that we bow quickly and rise slowly, "like a snake"[4] which, the rabbis said, loosened the spine and opened the body to the flow of divine energy.[5]

My own meditation practice, and the one taught in Minyan, derives from a Hasidic technique called *avodah be-bittul,* the discipline of self-annihilation. Avodah be-bittul is a meditation practice leading to the temporary ending of your sense of self and separateness. All definitions and labels are erased, and for a moment you discover yourself to be what you truly are: God's vehicle for knowing God as the Source and Substance of all reality.

The annihilation of self as a separate entity is essential to spiritual awakening. Your sense of separateness locks you into the one-sided view that the world of Yesh, the world of diverse and separate beings, is the only world. You are blind to the complementary reality of Ayin, the world of absolute oneness. You cannot awaken to Ayin while still in the mind-set of Yesh. Nor can you awaken to God while locked into the mind-set of Ayin. Remember, both Yesh and Ayin are manifestations of a Greater Unity. To awaken to the deepest truth you must awaken to yourself as both Yesh and Ayin without defining yourself as either Yesh or Ayin.

This is not an intellectual exercise. This is not something you can deduce logically from the facts at hand. The world you perceive while focused on self is the world of Yesh, the world of separate beings. When you practice meditation that world opens to the larger world of Ayin and for a moment you recognize that separateness and selfhood are relative and not absolute. Yes, you are a self, but no, that self is not permanent. As your meditation deepens, the self melts away, Yesh gives way to Ayin, and you may cling to the idea that you are nothing at all. But this too is one-sided. You are you but not only you. You are empty but not only empty.

Many meditative practices stop with the awakening of Ayin consciousness. They are content to take refuge in the egoless reality of absolute oneness. Judaism sees this not as an end, but only as another way station. There is a higher state yet to achieve, and that is the recognition of Yesh and Ayin as equal and necessary manifestations of the Greater Unity of God.

It is this state beyond both separateness and oneness that the Psalmist calls *kalta nafshi,* "the obliteration of my soul."[6] The medieval kabbalists called it *bittul she-me'ever le-ta'am va-daat,* annihilation beyond reason and knowledge, the ending of thought. Or, as Reb Nachman of Bratzlav teaches: "You cannot unite with God except by complete self-annihilation."[7] And complete annihilation means the annihilation of the idea of self as something and the self as nothing.

With the complete annihilation of self as Yesh or Ayin comes a renewed appreciation of Yesh and Ayin as complementary attributes of reality. The world is neither an illusion nor a snare; it is neither permanent nor worthless. It is simply what it is: the manifestation of God through the dual attributes of being and emptiness.

Your new understanding of reality as God in extension

returns you to the world of Yesh without losing your connection with Ayin. You see the myriad details of creation without imagining that they are separate from each other or the One from which they arise. You look at the world and yourself as expressions of God, united in a reality that makes for infinite diversity.

This understanding is accompanied by a heightened sense of connection with and compassion for all life; you sense a deep desire to bring about *tikkun ha-olam,* perfecting the world through love and justice.

The point of meditation as Judaism prescribes it is not to escape from the world, but to become a vehicle for perfecting the world, for bringing about its highest potential and soulfulness. Judaism is a profoundly this-worldly religion. Its overriding concern is to "perfect the world under the guidance of God."[8] You cannot perfect the world, however, if you insist on being separate from it. Trying to do so only traps you in projecting your own likes and dislikes onto the world. Perfection is not an imposition from without, but a nurturing of the holiness within. It is only when you see yourself and the world as one, and that one as part of the Greater Unity that is God, that you understand the true work of perfecting the world.

Perhaps the best understanding of the link between meditative self-emptying and world-perfecting was given to me by an ob/gyn nurse: "Minyan is like midwifery. The world and everything in it is trying to birth something wonderful, and I learn how to put myself aside and facilitate that birth. Meditation has profoundly affected the way I treat my kids, my husband, even my ex.

I don't impose my needs as much as recognize the differing gifts people bring to relationships. I mean, I'm not a pushover, but I see that even my desire to help can sometimes be a hindrance to another's growth."

Emptying of self and perfecting the world are two sides of the same spiritual practice. You are not seeking to escape the world, you are seeking to transform the world. You do this by recognizing the unity of all things in God and then acting accordingly.

When you awaken to this knowing you awaken to the fact that you were never asleep. Yesh is no less God than Ayin; God does not change. It is your perception of reality that changes. And the awakened human mind manages to perceive reality as both Yesh and Ayin, seeing God in both as both.

When you see all as God you no longer insist upon your absolute separateness, your absolute being. When you see all as God you see everything as empty of separate being; you are no longer apart from God, but a part of the Greater Unity that embraces duality. Your own separateness is lost and you are one with all and the One that is its Source and Substance.

This is how to practice avodah be-bittul. Sit comfortably. Relax your body. Do a mental check for points of tension and let them go. Typical tension points are the forehead, around the eyes, the jaw, and the stomach. Scan your body for tension, breathe slowly while focusing on the area of tension, and invite the tension to fade. While the cause of the discomfort may not leave, the physical expression of it can soften. This often allows you to deal with the cause more effectively, since the energy used to defend against it can be channeled toward resolving it.

Now shift awareness to your breathing. Proper breathing is central to meditation practice, and proper breathing means breathing from the diaphragm. The diaphragm is a muscle located underneath the rib cage. It separates the chest from the stomach. Breathing from the diaphragm allows you to breathe evenly and fully right into the lower part of the lungs.

When practicing meditation, bring your awareness to your breathing for a few moments. Do not interfere with it. Just watch the flow of the breath and the soft rise and fall of your stomach. Breathe evenly without gasps or breaks. Don't regiment your breathing, and it will soften of its own accord. The more gently the breath flows, the quieter the mind becomes. Whenever you find yourself agitated or ill at ease, focus on your breathing and return to that gentle flow. You will calm down and be better able to handle whatever it is that is upsetting you.

To maximize the effectiveness of your breathing you need to maintain a posture conducive to diaphragmic breathing. Some people choose to sit in a full lotus posture, with each foot resting on the opposite groin. Others choose to sit cross-legged, with each foot beneath the knee of the opposite leg. Still others prefer to sit in a straight-backed chair, with their feet parallel to each other on the floor. And some choose to lie on their backs to relieve the strain of sitting altogether, though most people find this position more conducive to sleep.

The point is to maintain a straight spine. Sitting with the

spine straight does not mean sitting with the body in a straight line. The spine curves naturally, being somewhat convex in the lower third of the back, the lumbar region, somewhat concave in the middle thoracic area, and convex again at the neck or cervical region. It helps to have someone observe your meditation posture to see that you are aligned properly. If you experience any pain while sitting—as opposed to mild discomfort—stop and try another posture.

There are many meditation aids available: benches, cushions, and pillows. Experiment and see which works best for you. Remember, the posture is held to help you with the breathing. If you are struggling to maintain the posture, you can be sure your breath is anything but slow and steady. Do what you must to sit comfortably.

When you simply sit and watch the mind at work—when you refuse to follow any thought or feeling, and allow all thoughts and feelings to rise and fall of their own accord—your mind slowly ceases its chattering. A deep quiet emerges and, for a moment at least, thought ceases. There seems to be no conscious activity in the brain; no thought, no thinker. Yet there is a profound knowing, albeit without a knower or an object that is known.

After a few moments of just sitting and observing what is happening, begin *gerushin,* the repetition of a holy phrase, which is described in the next chapter.

The purpose of repeating a holy phrase silently during meditation is to give the mind something to do. As soon as you begin your meditation your mind will clamor for attention. Thousands of thoughts and feelings will flood your conscious mind. Distractions by the dozens will seek to draw you away from your practice. Suddenly everything is more important than avodah be-bittul.

This chattering of your mind occurs whether you practice avodah be-bittul or not. The difference is that in avodah be-bittul you do not react to the noise. You simply observe it. Yet you can help the mind quiet itself with gerushin.

Returning the conscious mind to the repetition of a word or phrase gives the mind something to do without giving it anywhere to go, since the repetition does not generate linear thought. It does not distract the mind into replaying and analyzing the dramas that occupy it during the waking hours of your day. Like a baby sucking quietly on her thumb, the mind occupied with gerushin curls up into a comfortable corner and becomes still. When your mind wanders—and it will—don't fight it; simply bring your attention back to your silent repetition.

That is it. There is nothing magical in this. No visualizations, no affirmations, no fantasies to occupy the mind and thrill the heart. Just sitting, breathing, and silently repeating a holy phrase.

Can it be that simple? Yes, but do not mistake simple for easy. Try it and you will see that it is not easy at all.

Yet if you practice diligently, in a short while the benefits will become clear. You will be calmer, less stressed, less willing to identify with all the craziness around and within you. You will gain distance from your own desire for control and power and be better able to act in the world with justice and compassion.

It all depends upon your making avodah be-bittul a fixed part of your day. Each morning, ideally before you eat breakfast, set aside thirty minutes for meditation. If you wish to lengthen your meditation practice, add another thirty minutes in the late afternoon or early evening. In this way you will retrain the mind to see the world as it really is: the integrated, flowing wholeness of God.

GERUSHIN
Repetition

Gerushin is the silent repetition of a sacred word or phrase. Gerushin literally translates as "dispelling" and was used by the Hasidim to rid themselves of unwanted thoughts. In Minyan this practice is used to provide you with an ongoing meditation on God's infinite presence.

Repeating a sacred word or phrase as a means of meditation finds its earliest roots in the Bible. The Bible refers to this practice as *hagah*. In the book of the prophet Isaiah, for example, we read, "His heart shall meditate [hagah] terror,"[9] and in Psalms we find, "May the words of my mouth, the meditations [*hagayon*] of my heart, be acceptable to You, O God. . . ."[10]

That hagah is a verbal meditation is found in several other biblical passages: "The mouth of the righteous utters [hagah] wisdom";[11] "My tongue shall utter [hagah] Your righteousness";[12] "I will coo [hagah] like a dove."[13]

The Bible even hints at the notion of a mantralike practice when it says: "This book [referring most likely to some version of the Book of Deuteronomy] shall not depart from your mouth, and you shall meditate [hagah] on it day and night."[14] The Bible certainly seems to be promoting a practice of repeating the text over and over, either out loud or silently in your mind.

Centuries later, the rabbis picked up on this biblical hint and read meditative recitation into the dim past. According to rabbinic legend, Enoch, the father of Methuselah, was a master of this meditative technique. While the Bible tells us little of Enoch, the rabbis believed him to be a sandalmaker. According to the rabbis, as Enoch sewed each stitch to tie together the upper and lower parts of a sandal, he would say: *"Baruch Shem kavod malchuto l'olam vaed*/Blessed is His Name whose glorious kingdom is for ever and ever!" With this he was able to bind together not only the upper and lower parts of the sandal, but the upper (Ayin) and lower (Yesh) worlds as well.

The sentence ascribed to Enoch by the rabbis is the second line of the Shema, the central affirmation of Judaism: *Shema Yisrael Adonai Eloheinu Adonai Echad,*[15] which I translate as "Hear, O Israel, that which we call God is Nonduality Itself." The Shema is often repeated in meditation, though traditionally it is used this way only at bedtime.

When Rabbi Shmuel Bar Nahmeni would go down to the town of Eburra, he would stay at the home of Rabbi Yaakov the Miller. Once, Rabbi Zeira, Rabbi

Yaakov's son, wanting to learn all the holy ways and practices of the great rabbi, hid himself among the large baskets that were in Rabbi Shmuel's bedroom, in order to hear how he recited the Shema before going to sleep. That night he listened as Rabbi Shmuel said the Shema and repeated it again and again until he fell asleep while saying it.[16]

A similar practice was used by Joseph Caro (1488–1575), the Safed mystic and legalist most widely known for the compendium of legal rulings called the *Shulchan Aruch*. Rabbi Caro entered into nightly contact with an angel who revealed to him the deeper secrets of the Torah. His method for contacting the angel was the repetition of a passage of Mishna, the earlier part of the Talmud completed during the second century of the common era.

Rabbi Nachman of Bratzlav (1772–1810), the great-grandson of the Baal Shem Tov, popularized this meditative practice. Nachman saw the repetition of a sacred word or phrase as a mystical practice open to everyone. Indeed, he first introduced it as a remedial method of talking with God.

> If you cannot converse [with God] through formal prayer, but can say just one word, you should be strong-minded and say that one word many, many times, without end or number . . . until God, blessed be He, has compassion on you, and opens your mouth so that you can converse with Him freely.[17]

It is Nachman's version of this practice that came to be called gerushin, and it is upon his teaching of gerushin that our Minyan practice is based.

Gerushin relaxes the body and quiets the mind. It also detaches you from the immediacy of your feelings, allowing you to look at things more calmly and objectively and thus create a tranquil foundation from which to respond to life with ever-deepening sensitivity and compassion. To benefit from this simple spiritual tool you must repeat the phrase all day long.

In Psalm 150 we read: "Let every soul [*neshamah*] praise God."[18] Since the word "neshamah" (soul) derives from the same Hebrew root as the word *neshimah* (breath), the sages took the Bible to be saying that you should praise God with every breath. They taught this practice by encouraging those who wished to awaken to God to repeat the Aramaic phrase *B'rich Rachmana Malka d'Alma Marai d'hai Riga/*"Blessed is the Merciful One, Sovereign of the Universe, Master of this moment and Wholly Present" over and over, all day long.

The Hasidic rebbes further developed this teaching, adding other phrases for repetition and making it a powerful focal point of their daily spiritual practice. Rabbi Levi Yitzhak of Berditchev, for example, would immerse himself in God-consciousness by repeating *"HaRachaman"* (Merciful One) over and over without ceasing. Reb Nachman of Bratzlav taught the repetition of *"Ribbono shel olam"* (Master of the universe). Rabbi Yaakov Koppel was so famous for his repetition of Psalm 16:8—*"Shivitti HaShem l'negdi tamid/*I place God before me always"—

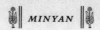

that even the Gentiles called him the *Shivittinik*. And Rabbi Alexander Ziskind left this instruction in his will as a means of encouraging his children to practice gerushin:

> And I will tell you, my beloved children, that whenever I was not involved in Torah or prayer, these three words (*Yotzri u'Bori Ata/* You are my Maker and Creator) and the acceptance of God, blessed be He, as my God, was ever-present in my mouth and even more so in my thoughts. Except for the forgetfulness which is part of human nature (according to God's will) . . . I can testify about myself, my beloved children, that there was not a minute during which my mind did not glory in God, blessed be His name and His remembrance forever, in the above language and language similar to it. Due to forgetfulness this would sometimes cease briefly from my mind, but it would immediately be rearoused—and all this due to my great love for Him, blessed be He.[19]

To practice gerushin you must find a sacred phrase or word with which you are comfortable. Here are some of the more commonly used Hebrew phrases for gerushin. I suggest you choose a phrase in Hebrew, though any language will do. Practicing gerushin in Hebrew has the added benefit of linking you to those sages who for thousands of years have found in the sound of Hebrew the power to quiet the mind and awaken to God.

Experiment for a few days with each of the phrases listed

here. See which seems most comfortable to you. Once you have made your choice, stay with it. The longer and more consistently a single phrase is used, the more power it has to train the mind toward silence. If you change phrases, your mind does not associate the phrase with stillness and will not give in to its calming power. Repetition is the key here, and repeating the same sound over and again without change deepens the effect.

- *Adonai/* Ineffable One
- *Shalom/* Peace
- *Baruch Ata Adonai/* Blessed are You, Ineffable One
- *Ribbono shel olam/* Master of the universe
- *Yotzi u'Bori Ata/* You are my Maker and Creator
- *HaRachaman/* Merciful One
- *Shivitti HaShem l'negdi tamid/* I place the Ineffable One before me always
- *Baruch Shem kavod malchuto l'olam vaed/* Blessed is His Name whose glorious kingdom is for ever and ever

Begin your gerushin by making the chosen phrase part of your daily meditation practice. Repeat it over and over again as you sit and follow the inhalation and exhalation of your breath. If you notice you have stopped the repetition, simply start it up again. During meditation gerushin helps keep your mind from wandering. Your normal waking-state consciousness is usually untrained and undisciplined. It picks up and runs with thoughts and feelings, leaving you exhausted mentally and physically.

Using gerushin in this way, you will experience moments of total emptying into God. Yesh gives way to Ayin, and then both give way to God.

> A person should be so absorbed in this practice that there is no longer awareness of self. There is nothing but the flow of life; all thoughts are with God. One who still knows how intensely goes the practice has not yet overcome the bonds of life.[20]

Through the silent repetition of a sacred phrase during meditation your whole "being is so absorbed that nothing remains of it at all; [there is] no self-consciousness whatsoever."[21] Yet gerushin should also be practiced outside the formal meditation of avodah be-bittul.

I find gerushin especially helpful when in a conflict situation. If, for one reason or another (or equally as likely for no reason at all), I find myself in an argument with someone, my mind is constricted; my breathing is short, rapid, and high in my chest. I am at war, and the prize is to prove a point that only moments ago did not matter to me one iota.

At times like these I am no longer repeating my sacred phrase. On the contrary, if there is any repetition going on in my mind, it is this: "I'll show you, I'll show you, I'll show you." As soon as I become aware that I am no longer practicing gerushin, I return my mind to it. Gerushin allows me to step back from what is going on both within and around me. Not that I become detached from life, but I become detached from my mind's chattering about life.

Immediately my breathing slows and deepens. My breath comes from deeper in my belly rather than higher in my chest. That relaxes me. My mind stops racing and my mouth stops babbling. I start to listen to what the other person is saying—not in order to formulate some witty response, but to learn what it is she or he is so passionate about. Even if the argument continues, the tone has changed. I am not so attached to winning. I am not so vehement in my speech. I can hear the other side even if I continue to disagree with it. I can make room for disagreement; I can make room for the other. The bottom line? I don't get as upset, and I often find common ground from which to effect resolution or at least move the conversation forward.

I do my best to practice gerushin continuously. As a result I am calmer, more focused, more centered, and less likely to be victimized by my ever-fluctuating thoughts and feelings. I do forget now and again, but as soon as I notice the repetition has ceased it starts up again almost of its own accord. You need not berate yourself if the repetition ceases. All you need do is begin again. You are not keeping score; there is no goal; you never start over; you just start again.

Gerushin can be practiced anywhere at any time. Caution should be taken when driving a car or engaged in some other activity that requires you to maintain vigilance, though some say that gerushin sharpens their sense of attention. The key is to get into the habit of repeating your sacred phrase.

Another remarkable benefit of practicing gerushin is that you can never waste time. I spend a great deal of time waiting in lines and in other people's offices, something I find physically and emotionally difficult. Yet when I look at these occasions as opportunities for gerushin I no longer see this as time wasted. And when the wait is over I am no longer agitated and annoyed but rested and refreshed, for I have used the time to center and quiet my mind and body.

The simple fact is gerushin works. Physically, it is soothing; as soon as I become aware of the phrase, my breathing slows and deepens, my body relaxes, and I smile. Emotionally, it is calming; as soon as I repeat the phrase, I find myself letting go of the need to control situations and people, which is at the root of so much negative emotional stress. Intellectually, it is freeing; repeating my phrase unhooks me from my ideas; I look at them more objectively, playfully, compassionately. Spiritually, it is fulfilling; when I repeat my sacred phrase, my sense of "I" lightens, the strain of maintaining a separate self eases, and I sense not that God is in me, but that I am in God.

MUSAR
Inspirational Reading

Musar is the name of a nineteenth-century educational movement that took root among the Jews of Lithuania. Founded by Rabbi Israel Lipkin Salanter (1810–1883), the movement focused on the reading of ethically inspirational literature.

While still a teenager, Israel Lipkin was recognized as a great scholar. Upon becoming a rabbi, he took the position of *mashgi'ah*, or spiritual mentor, and headed a yeshiva in Vilna. Rabbi Israel had very specific ideas as to how yeshiva life ought to be conducted and soon left his post to establish his own school. As his fame spread he began to deliver public lectures in Vilna, outlining his unique approach to ethical learning.

Rabbi Israel was convinced that Jews were suffering from a deep moral laziness. To combat this he proposed that the city's elite gather each Sabbath at a set time to discuss morals and personal growth. These gatherings, the rabbi believed, would attract others of lesser stature and eventually spread throughout the community.

During these meetings the rabbi urged people to speak softly, thoughtfully, and to concentrate on saying precisely what they meant. He discouraged joking, sarcasm, and irony and promoted the exploration of human nature. He hoped in this way to help the participants bolster their positive traits and reduce their negative ones.

Unfortunately these meetings never caught on, and the rabbi turned his attention from the elders to the children. It was among the yeshiva students influenced by Rabbi Lipkin that musar developed its unique methodology of invoking moral strength.

The central practice of yeshiva-based musar was the communal reading of inspirational texts. Students gathered at twilight to read. Oddly enough, there was no attempt to unify the reading or to focus on a single text. Each student was encouraged to read that which spoke to him most powerfully. What united the students was not a common text, but a common melody to which the text was recited. Rabbi Israel held that the melody would set the tone and mood for serious reflection and help the student retain the message of the text he was reading.

At first the students were encouraged to recite their texts for thirty minutes each day. As the movement grew, however, so did the time spent in musar recitation. Small groups of students would meet weekly among themselves to continue their recitation practice, and often several groups would join together for special recitation intensives. It became customary to practice the recitation in dim light to approximate the twilight suggested by Rabbi Israel and to encourage the need to focus on the text in order to read it.

In some yeshivahs a maximalist trend developed in which students read their texts for hours each day in the barest possible light. In these schools the student was also instructed in humbling exercises designed to weaken self-centeredness. A student, for example, might be sent to a drugstore to ask for an inappropriate item such as a hammer. Or he might be instructed to dress in rags and mingle with the wealthy people of the town. Or he might be asked to board a train without money or a ticket. In each instance the student was to experience the humbling effects of his situation and to monitor his reaction to minimize and eventually eliminate vanity, which was considered a major impediment to spiritual growth.

My own experience with musar practice was far less intimidating. Under the guidance of a musar rabbi in Jerusalem I learned to chant various English translations of musar texts to the tune of the Four Questions asked during the Passover seder. Rather than find the tune a helpful mnemonic for ethical study, however, I found it a terrible distraction. Having to fit the words to a melody for which they were not written meant I had to shift my attention from the meaning of what I was reading to the manner in which I read it. I had to shape each syllable to fit the tune, and more than once lost all attention to the message of the text.

Methodology aside, however, I did find the reading aloud of musar literature very helpful. There is something about reading out loud that helps one concentrate on the meaning of the text.

When creating the Minyan system of spiritual practice I naturally chose to include musar reading as part of the discipline. My own suggestion is to read for five to fifteen minutes each day without melody. To maximize the effectiveness of your reading, make it part of your daily meditation practice.

Dr. Herbert Benson, associate professor of medicine at Harvard Medical School and chief of the section on behavioral medicine at the New England Deaconess Hospital, has written extensively on the benefits of mixing meditation and focused reading as part of what he calls developing the "maximum mind." According to Dr. Benson, over the course of time your brain develops certain physical conduits that determine how you think, act, and feel. Dr. Benson calls these conduits "wiring." Your wiring can become so fixed as to make change nearly impossible.

Anyone who has tried to change a deep-seated habit knows this. Your best intentions are just not enough. You understand what needs to change; you have convinced yourself of the necessity for change; you may even have seen how without change your life may be threatened. Yet you do not change. Why? Because, Dr. Benson tells us, change is not a matter of will.

Habitual thoughts, feelings, and behaviors become hard-wired into your brain, and you cannot change them until you change the wiring. You have to make a physiological change to the brain's old wiring before you can successfully imprint new wiring. Fortunately you can make changes in the physiology of the brain's wiring, and avodah be-bittul is part of the process for doing so.

According to Dr. Benson, meditation softens the electronic pathways of the brain and allows you to establish new conduits. Meditation makes the brain more pliable. It releases the hold the old wiring has on your brain and allows you to imprint new pathways. By altering the way you think and act, you create new and additional connections in your brain that can, over time, come to dominate the old connections, helping to solidify the new thoughts and behaviors.

There are two stages to this rewiring process. The first is the deep relaxation brought about by avodah be-bittul meditation. The second is the focused reading that is our musar practice.

During meditation the two hemispheres of your brain begin to exchange information more freely, causing both hemispheres to function in sync with each other. When the right and left hemispheres are in sync your mind tends to operate more creatively, you process information more effectively, and you are capable of understanding things in different ways. Dr. Benson calls this "cognitive receptivity." Because you are more receptive to new information and new ways of thinking about old situations, you are open to alternative ways of handling situations. This openness allows you to make lasting changes in both mindset and behavior.

Traditional musar practice of chanting inspirational verse in dimly lighted rooms was an attempt to induce the meditative state and utilize its cognitive receptivity to help imprint the message of the text on the brains of the readers. Dr. Benson suggests a similar line of practice, urging his readers to follow their meditation with focused reading. The reading, he says, will engage the left hemisphere of your brain and begin to rewire it with new ideas more closely associated with the new thoughts, feelings, and behaviors you wish to engender.

In the context of Minyan, this focused reading is a contemporary version of traditional musar practice.

See to it that you learn from a musar book every day, and repeat what you have learned two or three times, either on the same day, or on successive days, and be sure that you get the lesson into your heart.[22]

After your thirty-minute meditation session, gently open your eyes and read for five to fifteen minutes or so from a positive, inspirational, and personally life-directing text. Read the text very slowly. Allow each word to establish itself in your mind. Welcome the message without engaging in an internal dialogue with it. This is not a scholastic exercise, but a continuation of the gentle meditative process of opening the self up to God, the Greater Whole of which you are a part. You may find that you cannot read more than a paragraph. Fine. Read the paragraph with full attention, and it will begin to plant seeds of personal transformation in your mind.

Following your reading, close your eyes and return to your meditation for another five minutes, thus allowing for a more successful reimprinting of the mind.

Whenever I present this part of the Minyan program people naturally ask for examples of what they can read. There are many fine anthologies of spiritually inspirational material. I do not think you have to limit yourself to Jewish material. Your aim is to find works that speak to you of the kind of person you wish to be and the kind of mind-set you wish to cultivate in yourself. These can be found in any and every religious tradition.

During the musar section of my seminars and workshops I provide participants with selections from the Book of Psalms and the daily prayer book from my own personal collection of musar texts. The translations from the original Hebrew are mine. As such, they are highly personalized and interpretive, and in no way pretend to be literal renderings of the originals. In my work as a poet and liturgist I seek to set forth the inner meaning the ancient Hebrew text invokes in me. The texts can bear many meanings, and I encourage you to explore many different versions of these texts, as well as to read them in the original if that is possible. Here is a selection:

Psalms

Psalm 29

The true God is beyond imagining.

The true God is Nameless.

The One who is All cannot Itself be any.

And yet this One who is nothing

speaks through all things.

Oceans rumble, thunder rattles,

great cedars fall with a crash—this is the voice of God

and this too God's silence.

Nations crumble under their own audacity.

People despair from their own greed.

This is the voice of God's justice:

no evil is prevented and no consequence softened.

We reap what we sow.

In the Temple all say "Glory!"

In the streets all cry "Chaos!"

Who can see the order in the whirlwind?

Who can see the pattern in the wildness?

Who dares cry "Glory" in the midst of chaos?

Still the heart and attend to Chaos;

Still the mind and the "Glory" is heard.

Still the soul and whisper "Amen."

In this there is salvation. In this and this alone.

___

Psalm 92

It is good to give thanks.

Does God need to hear my praise?

No. I need to express it.

To awaken to wonder, to holiness, to God

I must transcend the ego-centered drama

I pretend is life.

To shatter pretense give thanks.

Each thank-you reduces the false you.

When I give thanks I embrace others.

When I give thanks I move from drama to play

and discover the aliveness that Is

when I stop playing God

and discover that God is playing me.

It is good to give thanks.

for through thanksgiving awakening lies.

___

Psalm 93

The earth is secure;

it is I who imagine her frailty.

The earth stands firm;

it is I who plot her downfall.

She is greater than me,

and includes me in a larger scheme.

I am her child

though not her only child.

I am her hope

though not her only hope.

I am one she grew

to see her own face,

to know her own mind,

to foster surprise.

I am one who can know I am One.

———

Psalm 95

It is all You:

the valleys, the mountains

the shore and the sea,

it is all You.

And so am I—

This fragile reed

with beating heart and jumping mind;

this thinking bellows

breathed and breathing,

all You.

From You comes each

and to You each returns.

And in between is You as well.
You in anger and You in song,
You in play and You in pain,
You in danger and You in salvation;
it is all You and You are all it is.
I sing the wonders of all You are
and the simple truth of You is known.

—————

Psalm 96
Sing and awake.
Sing the never-before sung,
sing a new song
to God,
from God,
as God.
I still my mind
and calm my heart.
I soften my breath
and fill my belly with air.
I hold that fullness in tension
to be released only when the spirit moves.
My breath is transformed
from silence to sound,
from mystery to music
and back to mystery again.
For breath is the conduit to God,
and song the sound of breath in love.

Psalm 97

Embedded in my heart a melody beats
awaiting the conductor's call.
I hear it now and again, faintly.
It disturbs my quest for power
with hints of grace.
It haunts my dreams of control
with intimations of selflessness.
It stays my hand lifted in anger,
and calms my heart tight with rage.
It whispers to me of justice,
and sings to me of compassion.
It is the song of God and I shall sing it yet.
But not alone.
We each hear the song; we each need the choir.
Someday the song will rise in our mouths
and we will sing together in harmony.
Mountains of discord will melt before us,
idols of ego, tribe, and boundary will give way
as we weave a song of wonder
celebrating the many and the One.
Together we will sing the world awake,
bringing light to the dark places,
and letting the shadows dance once more.
Light is sown for the righteous;
joy for those who embrace it;
and song is a chariot to both.

Psalm 98

Sing to God,

for song is the highway to heaven.

Sing a new song,

for newness is the gift of humankind.

Sing to God a new song

whose words not yet written speak a joy not yet felt;

whose melody not yet composed

evokes a harmony not yet imagined.

Sing to God a new song.

To sing a new song I must sing with a new voice.

I must let go the known and embrace the unknown,

for the new is always surprise.

To sing a new song I must open myself to wonder.

I must embrace the fullness of mind and body.

I must immerse myself in the totality of Life,

its births and its deaths, its arisings and its passings.

I must let go the boxes into which I stuff the stuff of life

and allow what is to speak its truth.

And then I shall take that truth and sing it aloud.

With lyre and with drum, with voice and with silence

I will sing a song that surprises even God.

And in that surprise will be a great deliverance.

Psalm 99

The earth trembles with intimations of God.

The nations quake before the One without a flag.

Our boundaries shatter as the Whole hugs its parts.

We scar the earth with barbed lines

and define ourselves within them.

We label the stranger and mark a friend;

God is greater than this.

God is above our masks and our magic.

God speaks and there are no words.

God teaches and there are no books.

God guides and there are no gurus.

God plants justice and we sow discord.

God seeds compassion and we reap anger.

God extends charity and we shrug with indifference.

No wonder there is trembling.

We are frightened not of God but of ourselves.

We are frightened not of the One

but of the many we call "them."

May I make this day a day of emptying myself

of my self; a day of exalting the One

who is at the heart of the many.

May I make this day a day of humbling myself

before the One who is all.

And in this way will I move beyond fragmentation

to the greater unity

that is God's gift and my essence.

Liturgical Poems

There is a hunger in me no thing can fill;
a gnawing emptiness that calls forth
dreams dark and unfathomable.
My soul is whispering; Deep calling Deep,
and I know not how to respond.
The Beloved is near—as near as my breath,
as close as my breathing—
the World-Soul of which my soul
is but a part.
Let me run to it in love,
embracing the One who is me,
that I may embrace others who are One.
Enwrapped in Your Being
I am at peace with my becoming.
Engulfed in Your flame
I am clear and unclouded.
I am a window for the Light;
a lens through which You see Yourself as me,
and through which I see me as You.
How wondrous this One
Who is the root of all things.

———

Deep within me the Beloved stirs.
I smell her perfume;
I feel her touch;

I tingle with passion
that, once shared, becomes compassion.
Compassion for me, for you,
for those whom I have forgotten
and those whom I have yet to know.
With this love the world rebirths!
With this love I know—
Life embraces birth and death,
calm and struggle, joy and pain, you and me.
I open to the Beloved
arising within me,
swirling about me.
The Beloved is me
and I am the Beloved.
There is none else.

Listen! Israel, listen!
Still the mind's chatter, quiet the heart's desire.
The rush of life flows through me.
The heart of eternity beats in my own chest. Listen.
You are the fingers of a divine and infinite hand.
You are the thoughts of a divine and infinite mind.
There is only One Reality,
the Singular Source and Substance of all diversity.
This One alone is God.
Blessed is the One who manifests the Many.

Having heard the One I know myself commanded:

To love God,

the Source and Substance of All and Nothing,

with fullness of mind, body, heart and soul.

I shall feel freely and act wisely.

I shall let no opinion make truth taboo.

I shall be in the world with purpose and presence.

I shall set wisdom upon my heart

and share with her all who wish to learn.

I shall recite the oneness of God at home and away,

morning and night.

I shall glove my hands with compassion

and see that all my deeds are just.

I shall open my eyes to truth

and let my vision be daring and true.

I shall set righteousness upon the doorposts of my house

and upon my gates

that my going out and my coming in shall be for peace.

—————

I affirm this simple truth:

The Nameless One is the Source and Substance of All.

Creation is the Infinite manifest as the finite;

there is only the One, empty of form,

who fills all form.

Knowing this I let go of the compulsion to rule,

the desire to control others.

Rooted in this I learn to judge well,

uprooting oppression within and without.

God creates wonders

surpassing my understanding,

marvelous things beyond reckoning.

No science can fully know,

no dogma can even pretend to map

that which is beyond thought.

Yet it is God that sustains all things.

In God there is no faltering,

my every step is guided by forces beyond my ken.

Nothing is by chance,

for even chance keeps its own order.

The sages tell of hardened hearts

and bitter plagues—

the cost of freedom.

Remember well that cost and

make not light of struggle.

Let me mourn even my enemy's loss

taking no comfort in anyone's undoing.

For compassion is the Way, even as is justice.

When my ancestors beheld this they proclaimed:

Among all the gods we can name,

which compares to the One beyond naming?

Among all the quantities we can

label, number, mark, and measure,

which compares to the Truth at the heart of Reality?

My ancestors beheld the awesomeness of God:

"This is my God,
this Nameless One
is the Source and Substance of all.
This and this alone exists
throughout time and eternity."

———

May I live each day with fullness of mind,
attending to life and all she places before me.
Thus will I live without hesitation.
Only than can I lie down in peace,
having given life my all.
Only then can I rise up
in anticipation of a new day,
knowing I have so much more to give.
Let mercy refine my actions,
and justice shield me from enemies.
Let my life be a vehicle for grace and mercy,
bringing peace and comfort to all in need.
May the Source of Life spread a blanket of peace
over me, over Israel, over Jerusalem,
and over all the world.

———

The Eternal God
is not the God of Abraham
is not the God of Isaac
is not the God of Jacob

is not the God of Sarah

is not the God of Rebecca

is not the God of Leah

is not the God of Rachel

is not the God of my childhood

is not the God of my youth

is not the God of my adulthood

is not the God of my old age

is not the God of my dying

is not the God of my imagining.

The Eternal God is not my creation.

The Eternal God

is not the God who chooses

is not the God who commands

is not the God who punishes

is not the God who creates

is not the God who destroys

is not the God who makes me win

is not the God who sees that my enemies lose.

The Eternal God is not my creation.

The Eternal God is

the God who alone exists and who exists alone.

When I am free from ancestors,

free from traditions,

free from truths, free from words,

free from thoughts,

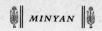

free from even the need to be free
there is God and there I am not.
Blessed in the One at the heart of my emptiness.

———

The One who is the many,
the Ocean who is the wave,
the Puzzle who is the piece
is God the Whole and Holy.

Creation is the dance of God in space and time.
I am the dance of God in this space and this time.
To awake to this is to awake from ignorance.
To awake to this is to awake from despair.
To awake to this is to awake from needless suffering.

May I find this day a rest from the sleep of fools.
May I find this day an awakening to the One
who is Whole and Holy;
Whole and wholly me.

———

For what do I pray?
For health?
For happiness?
For wealth or fame?
Who can say what will befall me?
I do what I do in pursuit of what I desire,
but only the hunt is mine;

the victory is in other hands.

I pray for nothing,

for I am nothing.

My desires are not Yours.

My needs are not Yours,

perhaps not even mine.

I pray simply to stand in Your presence.

I pray simply to stand and be present.

For that is all I can do:

stand and be present.

Present to You and what You bring

this moment and this moment again.

All there is is You;

Time and eternity, self and other—all You.

So I pray to pray.

I pray to be aware of the Being that is

all and nothing, here and there, now and forever.

———

Spirituality is living with attention.

Living with attention leads me to thanksgiving.

Thanksgiving is the response I have

to the great debt I accrue with each breath I take.

Attending to the everyday miracles of ordinary living

I am aware of the interconnectedness of all things.

I cannot be without you.

This cannot be without that.

All cannot be without each.

And each cannot be without every.
Thanksgiving is not for anything,
it is from everything.
May I cultivate the attention
to allow the thanks that is life
to inform the dance that is living.

———

Peace is not the absence of conflict.
Peace is dealing with conflict
while honoring justice.
Peace is not the absence of anger.
Peace is expressing anger
while honoring compassion.
Peace is not the absence of desire.
Peace is allowing for desire without
the fantasy that fulfillment brings happiness.
Peace is not the absence of fear.
Peace is knowing how to move through fear.
Peace is not the absence of self.
Peace is knowing that the self is absent.
May I cultivate the skills to live in peace:
to live with honor,
to live with justice,
to live with compassion,
to live with desire,
to live with fear,

to live with self,

to live with emptiness.

———

Let me attend to my words,

taking care to say what I mean

and do what I say.

Let me guard my tongue from evil

and my lips from speaking falsehood.

Let me rise above those who slander me,

and take care not to slander others.

Let me forgive those who offend against me,

and take care to offend only the unjust.

Let me open my heart to Torah

and find in her wisdom my way to righteousness.

———

I am loved.

Too easy to say, perhaps.

Too fleeting a feeling upon which to anchor a life.

And yet it is so.

I am loved. Though not always by me.

From my earliest days I was helped and guided

to find the path of justice, mercy, and humility.

Some guides were clear:

parents, grandparents, teachers, friends.

Some were subtle,

unexpected,

often painful.

They are all and always with me.

When I quiet my mind and still my heart

when I cease the nervous doing

that so often passes for purposeful living

I sense their wisdom

echoing in my heart.

I call out and hear the Echo

my voice no longer mine, and richer.

I listen and learn.

Through tales and tradition,

through law and acts of kindness

I find my way.

I take mitzvot upon myself

and seek to walk the path of righteousness.

They, too, become my guides,

and I think of them daily.

May I never withdraw my love from this path.

Blessed are they who love the way of Israel.

KAVVANAH
Attention

The Hebrew word *kavvanah* is a difficult one to translate and has had many different meanings over the centuries. Depending upon which period of Jewish history you read, *kavvanah* can mean meditation, concentration, devotion, intention, integrity of action, or attention.

The Talmudic sages use the word kavvanah in the sense of focused attention, especially during prayer, where the individual is to attend to the meaning of each word as a means of sensing the presence of God. The early Talmudic rabbis used to wait an hour before prayer in order to concentrate the mind,[23] but even they held differing opinions as to just how kavvanah was to be interpreted.[24]

Medieval sages continued the Talmud's concern with kavvanah. Bahya Ibn Paquda, one of the greatest mystics of the eleventh century, used to say: "Prayer without kavvanah is like a body without a soul."

The most famous of all medieval Jewish philosophers, Maimonides, says that "true kavvanah means freedom from all extraneous thought and complete awareness of the self within the greater presence of the Divine."[25]

Seeing in Maimonides' definition of kavvanah an affinity to avodah be-bittul, the annihilation of separate selfhood, the kabbalists built on his elimination of extraneous thought, taking him to mean the elimination of all self-focused thought. The kabbalists taught that when people pray they should attend so completely to the sounds of the words they utter (as opposed to their meanings) that they lose themselves in the sound and are no longer aware of themselves as separate physical beings.[26]

In the context of Minyan kavvanah refers to shifting your attention away from self to focus on the task at hand. Take washing dishes, for example. I prefer washing dishes by hand, rather than using the dishwasher. I love the warmth of the water on my skin; the slippery soap film that glides the brush over the dishes; the jarring, squeaky-clean sensation of a just-rinsed glass or plate. I am in no hurry when I do the dishes. I wash them simply to wash them. I don't dirty dishes in order to clean them, nor do I worry that almost as soon as they are clean someone is bound to dirty them again. There is no past or future in my washing. There is just washing. This is Maimonides' ending of extraneous thought and the discovering of the simple wonder of everyday activity.

Most of the time I am not so focused. Most of the time I dwell not in the world, but off to one side. My mind is occupied with a running commentary on what is going on and why it is going on. I am more like the sportscaster describing and providing color commentary to the events unfolding around me than I am like the athlete actually participating in the event.

Redirecting your attention from the doer to the doing requires you to slow down. If you are like most people, you are always rushing. It is as if there were a voice in your head forever urging you to hurry up. All this leaves you breathless, and breathless people are rarely spiritual people.

Breath and spirituality are intimately linked. The English word "spirit" derives from the Latin *spiritus,* breath. In Hebrew, *ruach* means both breath and spirit, while as I have already pointed out, neshamah, soul, shares the same root with neshimah, breath. By slowing the breathing and following the breath, you become more centered and awake. Yet your life probably leaves little time for such focused breathing. You gulp air as you gulp coffee and cola, and often for the same reason: to get enough energy to rush off to do the next thing.

A friend of mine works for a company whose motto is "Never stand still!" And she doesn't. She works at a frenzied pace, and the pace spills over into everything else she does. Her family is frantic, her play is frenzied, even her "down time" is rushed by her constant clock watching and her need to know whether it is time to get moving once again.

The very phrase "down time" is scary to me. Down time is a computer term, but you and I are not computers. Computers are either on or off. On, they are useful; off, they are useless. Down time on a computer is nonproductive, costly, and very frustrating. But "down time" for people is essential. If you do not make time to stand still, you will simply exhaust yourself physically, emotionally, intellectually, and spiritually.

"Yes, I know what you mean," one man said at a retreat I gave recently. "You are talking about burnout."

"It is a real problem in our office, I can tell you that," another added. "We make it a rule to recharge our batteries now and then."

The audience nodded in agreement. I shook my head sadly. "Burnout" and "recharging your batteries" are terms applicable to machines, not human beings. Using them in the context of human life shows how we have allowed ourselves to become adjunct to our technology.

I am in no way a Luddite advocating a return to a simpler world. On the contrary, I love technology. I am writing this book on the newest Macintosh computer. I am surrounded by phones, fax machines, and high-end stereo equipment. I use e-mail extensively and surf the Net daily. And I know that all of these devices actually speed up my sense of time. I am no longer content to wait a week to hear from someone through the mail. I e-mail a message and expect a reply within hours. Which means that I have to respond to that reply within hours as well, leaving me less time to think about what it is I should say.

Keeping up with our computers is exhausting and ultimately futile. The computer operates in a world of nanoseconds; you and I need hours, days, weeks, and years to develop. The more we try to accommodate ourselves to our machines, the more machinelike we become. We lose our humanity. We are too rushed to pay attention to what we are doing. We need an antidote to speed. That antidote is kavvanah.

Whenever I introduce the idea of slowing down and focusing, I see my listeners begin to cringe. "I knew it," someone inevitably complains, "I knew I would have to choose between living in the real world and this spirituality stuff. Well, I don't know about you, Rabbi, but I've got mouths to feed. If I slow down, I lose money, money I cannot afford to lose."

I understand that you will not abandon the high-tech life you have created for yourself in favor of a pastoral, meditative existence. Neither will I. Nor do you have to. Kavvanah can be used to punctuate your day with moments of attention that slow you down enough to maintain your humanity.

The first thing you must do is change the metaphor you

use for life. It is common to speak of life as a race. This is wrong and harmful. Where are you racing to? The end of life is death. Are you in such a hurry to get there?

Life is not a race; life is a symphony. The point of a race is to reach the finish line first; the point of a symphony is to enjoy what is taking place. Otherwise, as Alan Watts once said, the best symphony orchestra would be the one that played the fastest. The beauty of music of all kinds is that it follows a rhythm and blends notes with silence, beats with rests in a manner that makes each moment enjoyable.

A musical score without rests is noise. A life without rest is chaos. What you do with the practice of kavvanah is pace yourself and reintroduce moments of rest into your day, releasing the grip mechanical time has on your soul, allowing you to breathe like a person rather than pump like an engine.

How can you do this? The best plan is to set for yourself specific moments for kavvanah. As these become second nature to you, you may choose to add others. Even if you stick only to the basics suggested here, the pacing of your day will shift for the better.

Zen master Thich Nhat Hanh offers a good example for working moments of kavvanah into your life. When the phone rings, he suggests, stop what you are doing. Close your eyes for a moment and clear your mind. Focus attention on your breathing. (I would add that you also become conscious of the phrase you have chosen for gerushin and repeat it in sync with your breathing.) Let the phone ring three times. Remind yourself that if you choose to answer the phone, you have an obligation to the caller.

You must speak honestly, calmly. To be truly helpful you must not rush to judgment, but take the time to think matters through before you comment. Now answer the phone.

This same practice can be applied to other aspects of your life. Before eating, for example, close your eyes, focus on your breathing, turn your attention to the silent repetition of your sacred phrase, and allow your breathing to deepen naturally. The deepened breath will slow the mind and still the body. Breathe this way three times. Now open your eyes and attend to what it is you are about to eat. Notice the food's color and texture. Remind yourself of all that goes into producing this meal: the planting and harvesting, the shipping and processing. Before you eat take a moment to marvel at the fact that not a single thing on your plate could exist without the delicate balance of truly cosmic forces. It is amazing: the entire universe collaborates to feed you at this very moment! How can you not feel grateful, joyous, humble, and inspired by this simple truth? To eat without awareness of all that is happening is to waste a precious opportunity for awe and wonder.

Yet we do this all the time. When we eat, when we work, when we converse with others, there is always this subtle amnesia: we forget the wonder of what is happening. We get so caught up in the soap opera of our own selfish thoughts and feelings that we never really connect with what is going on. Kavvanah, slowing down to redirect your attention from doer to doing, acts as a corrective to all this.

Kavvanah can be integrated into anyone's day. When I am working on my computer, for example, I lose all track of time

Hours can go by without my getting up or talking with anyone. This is not healthy physically or spiritually. One way to deal with this is to program the computer to beep every forty-five minutes or so. At the sound of the beep I stop typing, push back from the keyboard, close my eyes, and breathe. I focus on gerushin for sixty seconds or so, then open my eyes and look about the room. I take note of my environment. Often I find something that needs doing: picking up fallen books or papers, watering a plant, dusting a shelf. I take a minute and do what needs doing and then go back to work. Every two hours I get up, step out of my office, and walk around for fifteen minutes, consciously practicing gerushin. I stop and talk with people or walk outside and notice the change in temperature, sunlight, and humidity.

I know people who program their wristwatches and their beepers in a similar fashion. A friend of mine has his beeper system set up so that every two hours he receives the message "Breathe, repeat phrase, attend." When the message comes he stops what he is doing, closes his eyes, and follows the beeper's advice for two minutes. "It returns me to the world," he once told me when explaining why he sets aside fixed times for kavvanah.

This is what kavvanah is about. The more cut off from the world you are, the more anxious and fearful you become. The weaker your awareness of how life conspires to bring you opportunities for meaningful doing, the stronger the fear that life conspires to defeat you. While I would be remiss to claim that isolating oneself in one's thoughts and feelings and cutting oneself off from the world is the basis for all neurosis, I do notice that

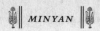

the more neurotic people are, the less linked they seem to be to the world around them.

Practicing kavvanah is not limited to working with technology. When you talk with someone, for example, you can enrich the quality of the conversation by focusing your attention properly.

When most of us enter into dialogue we do not really listen to what the other person is saying. We are always working on our side of the conversation. This requires us to focus on ourselves rather than on the person with whom we are speaking.

When we enter into a conversation with our side already formulated we are not engaging in dialogue. We are following a script. True conversation requires a serious element of unknowing. We don't know what the other person is going to say. We don't know what we are going to say. This not knowing makes us nervous. Indeed, waiting for someone to think things through before speaking can be awkward. But this does not mean it should not be done. Not knowing is essential to true dialogue. We have to leave ourselves open to what the other is saying, and in this there is no room for programmed responses.

The next time you are engaged in a serious conversation with someone, redirect your attention from what you want to say to what the other person is saying. Just listen. Focus on what is being said and how it is being said. Ask questions to clarify issues that are unclear. Gently probe the emotional state of the speaker; if you sense the speaker is upset or angry, ask her to verbalize this: "You're talking about this pretty calmly, but I get the feeling that you're really angry. Are you?" Collect as much relevant data from the speaker as you can, and then when it is your turn to speak—don't.

Take a moment to really ponder what you have heard. Breathe from the belly and let the words sink in. Remind yourself that you are connected to this person and to all life; that what you say can have implications far beyond what you intend or can foresee. Allow yourself to connect to the other person on the level of Ayin, the interdependence of all things. Now look the other person in the eye and speak.

Kavvanah is doing whatever it is you are doing with focused attention. People who practice focused attention discover the wonderment embedded in the simplest of acts. The more attention you pay to the things you do, the richer the doing becomes.

TZEDAKAH
Generosity

Tzedakah, from the Hebrew word *tzedek,* justice, is the most important commandment to which Jews are obligated: "Tzedakah is equal to all the other commandments combined."[27] In the Torah it is justice, and justice alone, that receives the double imperative: "Justice, justice you shall pursue."[28] Indeed, Torah holds even God to the strictures of justice. When Abraham confronts God over the destruction of Sodom, he challenges God with the ideal of justice: "Shall not the Judge of all the world act justly?"[29] Centuries later, when the prophets seek to lift Jewish civilization

to a new level, it is justice they hold as the ideal religious obligation: "Let justice well up as waters and righteousness as a mighty
stream."[30]

    This ancient concern for justice is infused into the daily
life of the individual through the practice of tzedakah, generosity.
Often wrongly translated as "charity," tzedakah is anything but.
Charity comes from the Latin *caritas,* meaning "from the heart."
Charity is a voluntary act motivated by your feeling another's
pain and finding in yourself the desire to help. Tzedakah, the
feminine form of tzedek, does not invoke feelings at all. Tzedakah
is a matter of justice and therefore a legislatable obligation. You
are obligated to be generous to those in need whether or not you
feel like it. One who does not give tzedakah to the needy is not
simply uncharitable of heart, but in violation of the law.

    Years ago while living in Jerusalem, I spent an afternoon
sitting with a group of beggars on a street corner. Over the course
of our conversation several beggars got up to leave. I was amazed
to see each of them give something to the others from his tin beggar's cup. When I asked about this they told me simply that
tzedakah was everyone's obligation, even a beggar's.

    The Torah requires Jews to give 10 percent of their earn-
ings to the poor every third year[31] and an additional sum annu-
ally toward the maintenance of the Temple and priesthood.[32]
When the Temple was destroyed in 70 C.E. the rabbis suspended
the priestly tax and increased the support for the needy. Hence-
forth Jews were to give 10 percent of their net income to the poor
each year.[33]

The importance of tzedakah never faded, and it was the hallmark of Jewish life for centuries.

> Life in the shtetl begins and ends with tzedakah. When a child is born, the father pledges a certain amount of money for distribution to the poor. At a funeral the mourners distribute coins to the beggars who swarm the cemetery, repeating, "Tzedakah saves from death."

> At every turn during one's life, the reminder to give is present. . . . Every celebration, every holiday, is accompanied by gifts to the needy. Each house has its round tin box into which coins are dropped for the support of various good works. A home that is not very poor will have a series of such boxes, one for the synagogue, one for a yeshiva in some distant city, one for "clothing the naked," one for "tending the sick," and so on. If something good or bad happens, one puts a coin into a [tzedakah] box. Before lighting the Sabbath candles, the housewife drops a coin into one of the boxes. . . .

> Children are trained in the habit of giving. A father will have his son give alms to the beggar instead of handing them over directly. A child is very often put in charge of the weekly dole at home, when beggars make their customary rounds. The gesture of giving becomes almost a reflex.[34]

Unfortunately, the obligatory, reflexive nature of tzedakah is less prevalent in our lives. Most of us are moved to give charity by images that play upon our emotions. The photograph of the starving infant; the vacant stares of the hopeless and helpless; the sights and sounds of poverty, tragedy, and despair: these tug at us. They won't let go until we do something, until we give something. So we give. Sometimes more, sometimes less. But the images keep on coming. We are overwhelmed by the need. We can impoverish ourselves and still not put a stop to the pain.

In response to this overwhelming need many of us become cold and unfeeling. We wear a mask of disinterest as we pass palms open for spare change. Or we concoct stories about how these desperate poor have done this to themselves. Or we rant about big business and how it does not care about people. Or about big government and how it does not care about people. Or about . . .

The one thing we try not to do is feel the pain and despair of people in need. How can we? There are so many desperate people, so many worthy causes, so many voices clamoring for our attention, compassion, and financial commitment. As one woman told me painfully: "If I gave to them, I would be robbing from my own children. I feel so guilty, but I don't know what to do."

Tzedakah is what to do. "The task is great. You cannot be expected to finish it, but neither are you free to ignore it."[35] Tzedakah is a middle path between apathy and self-impoverishment.

Whether you feel connected to those in need or not is not the concern of tzedakah. Whether you feel connected or not, you are part of a greater unity. You have an obligation based on that unity. Tzedakah is not something you have to feel like doing, it is simply something you have to do, period. Rather than wait to feel your connectedness with others before being generous, being generous can help arouse that feeling.

Tzedakah is the practice of generosity. When you practice generosity you open the circle of self and become aware of the larger whole in which the self rests. In time you recognize the interdependence of all beings, giving not out of pity, but out of moral obligation. It is the sense of obligation that maintains tzedakah's connection to justice. When giving tzedakah, know that "it is not really me who is giving, but God; I am simply the vehicle of transfer."[36] When receiving tzedakah, know that God is offering you an opportunity to live so that you may devote your deeds to goodness.[37]

While tzedakah may apply to a wide variety of generous acts, giving of your time and possessions as well as your wealth, it is financial giving that is its primary focus. The larger goal of tzedakah is the creation of an economically just and compassionate society where everyone has an opportunity to sustain him- or herself and where help is available for those who cannot do so.

The first thing you must do with regard to tzedakah is take an honest look at your financial situation. Can you afford to devote 10 percent of your income to tzedakah? If not, how much can you afford? Once you have settled on an amount, decide how you are going to set it aside. It is very difficult to pull much-needed money out of your regular savings or checking accounts for tzedakah. There is always another bill to pay or another purchase to make. If you are serious about tzedakah, you must separate tzedakah monies from your general operating budget. Determine how much money from each paycheck you can afford to devote to tzedakah, and deposit that amount in a separate tzedakah bank account. Draw your tzedakah funds from that account only.

In addition to setting aside a predetermined amount of money from your regular income, you can also collect a few extra tzedakah dollars by keeping a *pushke,* or tzedakah box, in your home. Display the pushke in a prominent place to remind yourself to drop loose change into it daily. When the box fills up you can add it to your tzedakah bank account or wallet. For decades Jews have traditionally kept a pushke in their homes to collect money for the Jewish National Fund (JNF), which uses the donations to develop forests in the State of Israel. You may wish to continue that tradition, and the JNF will be happy to supply you with the classic blue-and-white pushke. You may also expand on this practice by dedicating your home pushke funds for environmental projects.

Tzedakah can be given both to organizations and individuals. It can be a planned activity and a spontaneous one. When you are giving to organizations or helping to support causes you believe in, it is best to do so formally once or twice each year. In this way you can collect requests for tzedakah that come in the mail and weigh one against the other as you decide where best to spend your tzedakah dollars. Setting aside a specific time of year for this formal tzedakah allows you to consider a request without obligating yourself to fulfilling that request. Ask that information be sent to you and tell the person making the request when you will be making your decision.

Giving to individuals usually means giving spontaneously to people requesting your help on the street. Here, too, it is wise to do some planning. Determine how much of your tzedakah budget will go to this kind of giving. Then carry some of this money with you daily in a separate tzedakah wallet or purse. When someone asks for money take it from that wallet. When the wallet is empty you know you have met your tzedakah obligation. If you can and wish to give more, you may, but you do not have to feel guilty if you cannot, knowing that you have done what is just.

Many people are leery of giving money to people they suspect may use it for alcohol or drugs. Instead you can offer food or food certificates redeemable at local restaurants. Your local shelters may also have coupons you can buy that are redeemable for a night's shelter. In my congregation we encourage people to carry nonperishable foodstuffs in their cars to share with people asking for food at traffic lights.

No mention of tzedakah would be complete without reference to Maimonides' eight levels of tzedakah. For centuries this has been the Jew's guideline for giving, focusing not on the amount given (which is fixed by law at 10 percent), but on the attitude of the giver. Beginning with the least virtuous and progressing to the most, Maimonides lists the following:

- giving grudgingly
- giving less than is fitting, but with good humor
- giving only after being asked
- giving before being asked
- giving without knowing who receives
  (so as not to embarrass the recipient)
- giving anonymously
- giving so that both donor and recipient are
  anonymous
- helping the needy become self-sufficient

Maimonides' focus on the donor often surprises people. Doesn't it matter to whom you give tzedakah? Are all recipients equal? Should we give without regard to whom we give? At one Minyan retreat this issue sparked a lively discussion.

About one-third of the participants insisted that since tzedakah money was limited it should be used where it could do the most good. "We should focus our dollars on doing things to help people become self-sufficient. And that means giving to programs that help people who have the desire to become self-sufficient." This group argued against giving to people on the street and in favor of supporting projects like halfway houses, where the people are making an effort to "get their act together."

An almost equal number of people offered a very different view. "This has nothing to do with the recipient. Maimonides is not outlining a social welfare program, he is talking about tzedakah as a spiritual practice. The practice is to give without judging and without using the gift for self-aggrandizement. It doesn't matter where your money goes as long as it goes. Maimonides is concerned with the mind-set of the donor; the recipients are almost secondary. The point is to give without judging."

There is something of value in both positions, and the participants wrestled with this problem for quite a while without fully resolving the issue.

In Maimonides' time organized aid to the needy was run by the community as a whole, and judging the poor was almost unheard of. There was no thought that the poor have somehow chosen their plight. On the contrary, there was a general assumption that people want to take care of themselves but that sometimes doing so without the help of your neighbor is impossible. Maimonides focuses on the giver because the recipient was assumed to be blameless. More tellingly, however, he strives for anonymity between donor and recipient because it is likely that the two already know each other; the helpless were not strangers to the helpers.

This is a very important point. What separates our world from Maimonides' is not the enormity of the problem, but the anonymity of the poor. In centuries past tzedakah went to help your neighbors; today it goes largely to help strangers. And there is a suspicion that accompanies any dealings with strangers: Are you being taken advantage of?

The spiritual challenge of contemporary tzedakah practice is to overcome the problem of the stranger. We must move beyond the sense of separation we often feel when dealing with the poor. "Do not mistreat strangers, for you yourselves were strangers in Egypt."[38] Because of this I suggest that we no longer take Maimonides' list literally. While it is always good not to use donor status for self-aggrandizement, it may no longer be good to maintain the anonymity of donor and recipient.

Professional fund-raisers know this to be true. They try to personalize the plight of their cause. The entire goal of having a "poster child" is to give a face to the stranger on whose behalf funds are being raised. Often this technique is used simply to play on your emotions, but, as we have said, that is because charity is a financial response to an emotional pull of conscience. Tzedakah is not charity.

You give tzedakah because it is the right thing to do, whether or not you feel like giving. So there is no need to play on your emotions. You need to put a face and a name to the stranger because you must overcome the very idea of stranger and reclaim the lost sense of neighbor. This is the real spiritual side of tzedakah. Tzedakah is not the practice of being nonjudgmental, it is the act of recognizing neighbors.

How do you go about doing this? Make eye contact with people asking for money on the street. Look past their attire and remind yourself that they, like you, are manifestations of God. Smile. Say something pleasant. Take care not to sound condescending. Do not speak to the poor as if they were little children. Treat them respectfully.

"This all sounds so good, Rabbi," someone almost always says, "but the fact is if I spoke to every poor person I pass on the

THE TEN PRACTICES OF MINYAN

street, I'd not only be broke myself, but I'd never get to where I have to go."

Taking these things to extremes is a common way of excusing yourself from having to do anything. I understand that you may be confronted with dozens of homeless people daily. You cannot help them all. You don't have to. All you have to do is give tzedakah according to your budget. You can choose to focus on the same one or two people each day, or you can choose different people each day. The issue is not whether to give—tzedakah says you have to give—the issue is how to give. Give in such a way as you begin to recognize these people as your neighbors.

Tzedakah is not about power or poverty, but about recognizing the interdependence of all things and our obligation to each other to help create the most just world we can.

Jewish tradition has linked many daily activities with the giving of tzedakah. In this way the rabbis hoped to make the giving of tzedakah a habit. Here are some of the more practical ones. Put money in a pushke or add it to your tzedakah wallet

- before you eat a meal
- before making love
- before you go food shopping
- before you go clothes shopping
- before lighting Shabbat candles
- before going on a journey

- before a friend leaves on a trip, for her to donate during her journey

GEMILUT CHESED
Kindness

Gemilut chesed, which translates literally as the "bestowal of loving kindness," first appears as central to Jewish life in a maxim attributed to the Talmudic sage Simon the Just: "The world stands upon three things: Torah, temple service, and acts of loving kindness."[39]

People often confuse gemilut chesed with *mitzvot.* Mitzvot are laws derived from the Torah and expounded by the rabbis in the Talmud. Acts of gemilut chesed are acts of kindness that are not legislated, but which are vital to the well-being of any community. The nature of the confusion arises from the misuse of the word "mitzvah" to mean a good deed. There are mitzvot that are good deeds, but not all mitzvot fall into this category.

For example, it is a mitzvah to feed the hungry and to give tzedakah. It is also a mitzvah to place fringes on the corners of your garments and to wear no clothing that mixes linen with flax. While the quality of these mitzvot differ substantially, their status as divine commands is equal.

The fundamental difference between mitzvot and gemilut chesed is that mitzvot can be fixed and regulated, while acts of loving kindness have "no fixed measure."[40] In other words, unlike the 10 percent limit of tzedakah, acts of kindness need not be limited in amount or duration.

> Tzedakah can be given only with one's money; gemilut chesed, both by personal service and with money. Tzedakah can be given only to the poor; gemilut chesed can be given to both the poor and the rich. Tzedakah can be given only to the living; gemilut chesed can be given both to the living and the dead.[41]

Historically, gemilut chesed has focused on honoring your parents, promoting harmony between people, offering hospitality to travelers, visiting the sick, providing a dowry for an impoverished bride, and caring for the dead. With regard to the latter, the ancient rabbis joked that this act alone is pure kindness, since only here is the bestower of kindness certain that the recipient will not return the favor.[42]

Throughout the centuries, gemilut chesed was a deciding factor in measuring the quality of one's Jewishness. Indeed, the rabbis even went so far as to question the Jewishness of one who did not practice gemilut chesed.[43] Spiritually, too, gemilut chesed was of central concern: "One who engages in Torah study and does not involve himself in doing deeds of kindness is like one who has no God."[44]

The nineteenth-century sage Rabbi Israel Meir HaKohen, called the *Hafetz Hayim* after the title of his most famous book, taught: "You occasionally see a Jew learning as much Torah as he can. He values his time and does not waste any for fear he will not study as much as he should. But if he does not set aside part of the day to do deeds of kindness—he is a fool!"[45]

Traditionally, gemilut chesed refers to acts of kindness performed with no thought of reward. One classic example is donating money to help bury an indigent person. You do it because it is right, knowing that you will receive no reward for your action. While certainly not limited to or even centered on financial matters, historically the principle of gemilut chesed often involved the exchange of money.

Torah forbids Jews from charging interest on money loaned to other Jews.[46] The world of the Torah was largely agrarian, and money was not an essential part of daily survival. Loans were rarely needed, and when they were they had to be interest free. As Jewish civilization evolved into a more urban-based economy, the nature of loans had to change. The rabbis created a legal fiction to get around the Torah's agrarian-based restrictions. They invented a category called *heter iska,* or "permission to do business." Under this category people could lend money to businesses or investors and thereby become partners in the business or investment. As partners they were allowed to recoup their investment and make a profit from it.

Heter iska is limited to business transactions. Any money lent to persons in need is still interest free. To meet the needs of the poor for these loans, almost every Jewish community sponsors a free loan society. In Miami I know of two such societies, one of them run by my own congregation.

Our free loan society is governed by a board of five members drawn from the congregation. People apply for help to cover rent, food bills, medical expenses, and other basic needs. The money is lent without interest and with the expectation that if and when the recipient can repay the loan he or she will do so. When the money is returned it is loaned out again. While the fund is of a fixed amount with a cap on the size of each loan, it has served the needs of our community quite well, helping people through financially difficult times without the embarrassment of charity or the further financial burden of interest payments.

Financial aid is just one focus of gemilut chesed. Visiting the sick (*bikkur cholim*) and hospitality (*hachnasat orchim*) are also traditional acts of loving kindness.

Rabbi Helbo fell ill and none of the sages visited him. Rabbi Kahana rebuked the sages, saying: "Did it not once happen that one of Rabbi Akiva's disciples fell sick and the sages did not visit him? Rabbi Akiva himself visited him, and because [he saw to it that the floor] was swept and washed, the sick man recovered. "My master," he said to Rabbi Akiva, "you have revived me." Rabbi Akiva went out and taught: "One who does not visit the sick is like one who sheds blood."[47]

This story illustrates how powerful a visit to the sick can be. Just knowing that people care about you can help you recover. Thus the rabbis taught that whoever visits the sick removes one-sixtieth of their illness, while one who fails to visit the sick hastens their death.[48] Notice, however, that Akiva did not simply visit the sick person, but saw to his needs as well. Gemilut chesed requires you to place others first, to see what needs to be done, and to do it.

It is unfortunate today that visits to the sick in hospitals are often left to clergy. While some people enjoy the company of their rabbi, many are intimidated by such a visit, fearing that if they are sick enough to merit the visit of the rabbi, maybe they are too sick to recover. Visiting the sick is an obligation placed on all Jews and should be a regular part of your Minyan practice.

My congregation (and, of course, many others) has a Bikkur Cholim Society, a group of people who share the responsibility of visiting the ill both in their homes and at the hospital. The group is made up of volunteers who go through a short but intensive training session with therapists, social workers, and hospital staff. The purpose of the training is to help the volunteers learn what they can and cannot do and what they should and should not say during their visits.

When we learn of someone who is ill, we call to see if he or she would like visitors. If the answer is yes, we contact the Bikkur Cholim Society, which works out its own schedule. While the society does not replace the need for rabbinical visits, it does broaden the scope of gemilut chesed practiced by our congregation.

It is also expected that whenever a Jew hears of another's illness he or she should offer a prayer for healing. Spontaneous prayer is often alien to modern Jews, yet the desire to say something remains. To help with this my congregation created a small laminated card with a healing prayer on one side and a prayer for someone who has died on the other. The healing prayer we use is this:

> May the One who blessed our ancestors Abraham, Isaac, Jacob, Sarah, Rebecca, Rachel, and Leah bless _____ as well. May s/he whose life is gripped by suffering open to the fullness of this moment. May s/he discover through pain and torment the strength to live with grace and humor. May s/he discover through doubt and anguish the strength to live with dignity and holiness. May s/he know that God is All and in this way come to a healing transformation of body, mind, heart, and soul. Amen.

Such a formal reading may be too much for you. The shortest prayer in the Torah is one offered by Moses on behalf of Miriam, his sister: "O Lord, please heal her."[49] Whatever words you choose to use, it is part of your obligation as a human being to say something.

Visiting the sick may mean that you are present when a person dies. Often something needs to be said to mark the enormity of this moment. Most of us are at a loss for words at such times, and while silence is initially the most appropriate response, after the first moments of tears and stunned silence the people present feel a need to say something.

At Beth Or we use the following prayer when in the presence of death or with people who did not have a chance to say anything at the moment of death and who wish some sense of closure regarding it.

I/we acknowledge the impermanence of life and accept with all humility the stark simplicity of death. As a wave returns to the ocean, so has _____ returned to God. There is no loss, but there is a great ache. There is no break, but there is transformation.

May I/we discover in the emptiness of self the true nature of all things as expressions of God.

On behalf of _____ I/we ask forgiveness from all s/he may have hurt. May her/his death atone for her/his mistakes and may s/he be remembered for goodness.

On behalf of _____ I/we bestow forgiveness upon all who have hurt her/him that s/he might let go the past and embrace eternity.

From God we arise; to God we return; blessed is the endless creativity of God.

Another traditional focus of gemilut chesed is hachnasat orchim, hospitality. Your home may well be your castle, but do not surround it with a moat. Open your home to your neighbors, and, when appropriate, welcome strangers as well.

The Talmudic sages underscored the importance of hospitality by ascribing the fall of Jerusalem to the Romans in the year 70 C.E. to the lack of hospitality among her residents:

> A certain man had a friend named Kamtza and an enemy named Bar Kamtza. The man held a huge feast for his friends and ordered his servant to invite his friend Kamtza. By mistake the servant invited the man's enemy Bar Kamtza.
>
> When the latter arrived at the feast the host accosted him, demanding that he leave. Bar Kamtza begged him not to do him such an indignity, and offered to pay the man for whatever food he would eat. The man refused. Bar Kamtza then offered to pay for half the banquet if he would be allowed to stay. Again the man refused. In desperation, Bar Kamtza offered to pay for the entire banquet if only he be spared the embarrassment of having to leave. The host responded by having Bar Kamtza forcibly removed from the feast.
>
> Bar Kamtza was humiliated and angry. The room had been filled with sages and rabbis, and not one came to his defense and the defense of hospitality.
>
> He went to the Roman emperor and convinced him that the Jews of Jerusalem were plotting against him. The city was destroyed by the Romans shortly thereafter.[50]

Hospitality is essential to spiritual practice. It reminds you that you are part of a greater whole. Gemilut chesed is about putting others first. Putting others first puts you in the midst of life without the illusion of being the center of life.

Everything you have—your clothes, your food, your car, your home, your job, your family, the very thoughts you think—are, in one way or another, dependent upon the labor and love of others.

> Ben Zoma used to say: When about to eat bread ponder: What labor Adam had to carry out before he obtained bread to eat! He plowed, he sowed, he reaped, he bound, he threshed and winnowed and selected the ears, he ground and sifted, he kneaded and baked, and then at last he ate. Whereas I get up and find all these things done for me.[51]

When you do stop to ponder you cannot help but be grateful for all that is done for you. Therefore our sages taught that it is forbidden to enjoy anything in this world without first reciting a prayer of thanksgiving.[52]

So many things are given you that the enormity of your debt is overwhelming. It cannot be repaid, nor can it be ignored Gemilut chesed is the act of working off a little bit of this cosmic debt by engaging in acts of kindness and treating everyone and everything with utmost respect.

My friend and teacher David Reynolds, the founder of Constructive Living, tells of an effort he made to pay back some of his debt. David lived in a fairly run-down section of Los Angeles. On the street corner was a gas station, and next to it was a vacant lot. The lot belonged to the gas station but was unused and littered with trash.

To repay some of the debt he felt he owed his community, David asked the gas station manager if he could clean up the lot. At first the man feared this was some kind of scam. After David convinced him otherwise, David set a date for the cleanup and left.

On the appointed morning he showed up and began filling trash bags with refuse. It was hard, backbreaking work. The station manager took pity on David and brought him a broom handle on which he had affixed a nail. At least David wouldn't have to bend over so often. Of course the station manager's help only added to David's debt, but he was grateful for the stick. Not long after, David noticed that the manager had fashioned a second stick and was himself picking up trash in another corner of the lot. His debt deepened. Passerbys could not help but notice the two men, and they, too, began to pitch in. People came out with ice-cold drinks, more sticks and trash bags, and additional helping hands. It became a community cleanup.

The lot did get clean, but David's debt had grown. That is the nature of gemilut chesed: the more kindness you do, the more kindness you evoke in others, and your obligation to them grows. It is this mutual obligation in giving, caring, and kindness that gives gemilut chesed its power and makes it a deeply spiritual practice.

Gemilut chesed transforms your life from one of taking to one of giving and receiving. Recognizing the quality of receiving puts you in need of reciprocating for the many gifts that come to you each day.

Gemilut chesed is a wonderful practice. By putting others first, you discover how much others do for you. By putting others first, you find that you are not a limited and isolated individual in competition with others. By putting others first, you discover that you can make the world just a little brighter for your having been born into it.

Several members of my congregation have applied gemilut chesed to social projects. One woman took upon herself the obligation of establishing a neighborhood CrimeWatch as an expression of helping others. Another formed a series of safe houses in her neighborhood where local children in need could come for help.

Not all acts of kindness, of course, require such great effort and dedication. When you go to a bank, for example, speak pleasantly to the bank teller; when you purchase something from a store, talk kindly with the person behind the cash register. These people provide you with a service. They make your life a little easier. You owe them something in return. Kindness is the primary currency needed for this type of exchange.

A friend of mine makes it a habit to drop a quarter in a parking meter that has expired to save the car's owner a ticket. Every once in a while the car's owner sees him do it. "The look of shock at this simple act of kindness both saddens me and makes me glad. I'm glad I could help, but I am sad that such acts are so rare."

Pick a person close to you and do something special for that person. Give a single parent the night off by offering to take care of the children for an evening. Hold doors open for people; offer to help people who look lost; say "please" and "thank you"; smile at people—these can go a long way to making everyone's day a little nicer.

One of the most effective acts of gemilut chesed is to write thank-you notes to helpful people. Keep a stack of stamped note cards handy and use them regularly. I write to store managers, to authors of books that have moved me, even to friends now and again. In a similar vein, praise helpful employees to their managers; most people hear only complaints, but praise is the more effective way of letting people know what really matters. David Reynolds suggests we say "thank you" at least ten times each day. It is a good number for Minyan practice as well.

Gemilut chesed should not be limited to people. Take care of the things that take care of you: hang up your clothes; wash your dishes; do your laundry; clean your house; maintain your car. You cannot function nearly as well without these things. Show them respect and kindness by treating them properly.

I learned this in a most unusual manner. Several years ago I needed to resole a pair of Rockport dress shoes. The best way to do this is to send the shoes to the manufacturer, which I did. The shoes were returned with new soles, a wonderful new shine, and a handwritten letter from the person who did the work.

"Dear Rabbi Shapiro," the letter began. "We at Rockport take great pride in the quality of our work and our product. It is clear to me from the condition of your shoes, however, that you do not. The backs are cracked from improper use [I kick the shoes off without untying them]; the leather is dry from insufficient cleaning and polishing; and the overall look of the shoe is sloppy. On behalf of all of us who work hard to offer you a quality product, I wish you would take better care of our shoes." The letter was signed and came with a shoe-polish kit complete with just the right shade of polish.

I still kick my shoes off now and again, but I am much more kind to them than I ever was before. I am forever indebted to this wise teacher for reminding me of the importance of gemilut chesed with regard to the things in my life. Don't wait to receive a letter of reprimand. Do the right thing on your own.

PITRON CHALOMOT
Dream Interpretation

Pitron chalomot is Hebrew for dreamwork: using your dreams as vehicles for exploring the direction your life is taking. In rabbinic literature dreams are said to be "one-sixtieth prophecy," and the Zohar, the "bible" of mystical Judaism, tells us that "nothing takes place in the world without having previously been made known by means of a dream. . . ."[53] My understanding of dreams comes from the sixteenth-century sage Rabbi Solomon Almoni and his book *Interpretations of Dreams,* which was published in Salonika in 1515. The book has gone through many printings over the last four hundred years and is even cited by Sigmund Freud in his *Interpretations of Dreams.*

Almoni sought to provide his readers with principles of dream interpretation that make clear the message and meaning the dream seeks to convey. Nevertheless he recognized that there is no one right way to interpret a dream. Indeed, from the perspective of Minyan your goal is not to uncover the one true interpretation, but to entertain as many interpretations as possible, even if they are contradictory. Dreams are used to stimulate your thinking about your life, how you are living it, and where it is going.

Years ago an elderly woman came to me with a haunting dream. She was dead and lying in a coffin in a chapel. It was her funeral service. She could hear what was being said but could not see anything. The rabbi asked people to come up to the coffin and say good-bye to her. No one came.

She had had the dream several times over a period of two weeks. It upset her greatly. The woman asked to see me and came to her appointment accompanied by her daughter. The two of them sat together on my office sofa while the mother related her dream.

"I just don't understand it, Rabbi. Why didn't anyone come to say good-bye?"

We talked a bit about what was happening in her life. Her husband had died about seven months ago. She was well taken care of financially; her only problem was isolation.

Again she asked plaintively: "Why didn't anybody come?"

Suddenly her daughter cried out: "Mother! Don't you see? Don't you get it? Nobody comes because you have cut yourself off from everybody! Ever since Daddy died you've been hiding in the house. People call and you don't want to talk. They leave messages and you don't return them. They invite you to go out or they ask you to visit, and you refuse to go. How long will people keep trying? Not long, Mother. Everybody is tired of it, and so when you die it won't matter to anyone. My God, Mother, you're almost dead now. . . ."

Her voice trailed off and was replaced by quiet sobbing. Her mother just stared at her, wide-eyed and embarrassed.

"When did you die?" I asked the woman.

"February thirteenth, this year," she answered in a dull, hoarse whisper.

"No," I said. "That is when your husband died. I asked you when you died. That is what the dream suggests, isn't it? That you have died?"

The woman looked shocked. "Oh my God," she sighed. "Oh my God." Then she too started to cry.

It was true. She had died when her husband died. She had isolated herself at home no less effectively than he was isolated in the grave.

"Don't dismiss the dream or interpret it away," I said to her as she prepared to leave. "Listen to it. Think about it. What is it saying about the quality of your life; about where your life is heading? Remember, dreams are signposts hinting at possible destinations suggested by your present course of action. You need not end up where the dream suggests, because you can change course anytime."

I bumped into the daughter several weeks after our meeting, and she told me that her mother had been shocked and shaken by her meeting with me. "But it worked. She went home that night and called three friends. It took a while longer for her to go out, but she started building bridges right away. She still misses Dad, of course, we all do, but at least she is alive again."

The more you work with your dreams, the more layers of meaning you will find. Pitron chalomot is about uncovering these layers and allowing them to highlight issues and forces at work in your life. There is no set procedure for this, though I suggest some guidelines to aid your practice.

When you go to sleep ask yourself to remember any dreams you may have. If you wake from a dream or if you wake up in the morning with a dream still lurking at the fringes of consciousness, lie still with your eyes closed. Allow the dream to become more vivid. Keep a dream journal, a small flashlight, and a pen by your bed, and write the dream down in as much detail as possible. Some people find writing awkward and prefer to use a tape recorder. Either method works, though it is wise to transcribe the dream from the tape to paper to facilitate working with it.

When first reading a dream, do so only to clarify the plot. Read the dream as a short story, no matter how bizarre it is. Read the dream again and look for nuances: Why does the dream use the images it does? How might the dream's dialogue, location, and characters connect to your waking life? If you dream of Aunt Fanny, is it really her? Did you talk with her yesterday? Are you replaying real events in the surreal world of the dream, or does she stand for something more?

When you are satisfied you understand the plot and have placed the dream in the context of your everyday life, play with the text. What could it mean? Even if you did just meet with Aunt Fanny, what is it about her that her presence in your dream might symbolize? Ask trusted friends to suggest other interpretations. You are looking not for continuity of meaning, but simply for an abundance of options. Allow these to percolate in your mind and see if you begin to get a sense of what you might learn from the dream. All meanings are relevant if they help you understand the implications of your behavior.

Finally, look to see if the dream contains some unexpected insight, arising not from the conscious self, but from the unconscious self or soul. This is dream as prophecy, when prophecy is taken to mean a message from the deeper unconscious, revealing the forces at work in your life of which the ego is largely unconscious. There are no words to describe these insights, but an example may help make my point.

A friend's mother was dying of cancer. She was in the hospital and despite medication was in terrible pain. She believed that she was without hope and cursed each moment of life left to her.

One night she dreamt that a hand extended down to her from heaven. The hand offered her a wreath, green and leafy. In her dream she sat up (something she could no longer physically do) and took hold of the offering. As soon as she touched the wreath she felt a healing energy flow through her. She was still dying, but all of a sudden she was living.

She awoke calm and peaceful. Her body was near death, but her spirit was brimming with life. When her family arrived at the hospital she greeted them warmly. They talked, they smiled, they prepared each other for her imminent passing.

This is the deepest level of pitron chalomot. She did not interpret her dream, she was transformed by it. I wish the story ended here. Unfortunately it does not. Her rabbi arrived to see her later that day. She told him the dream, expecting validation and joy at her having found peace. Instead: "What nonsense," the rabbi said. "Don't put any stock in such dreams. They are the result of all this medication you are taking."

She knew he was wrong but couldn't hold on to her truth. Her peace was shattered, the pain returned, and she died in agony.

You must be careful when commenting on the dreams of others. Do not impose your personal beliefs or theology on other people, but open to the dream without preconception. As the Talmud puts it: "All dreams follow the mouth."

There were twenty-four interpreters of dreams in Jerusalem. Once I dreamt a dream and I went round to all of them and they all gave different interpretations, and eleven were fulfilled, thus confirming that which is said: All dreams follow the mouth.[54]

How do we know when an interpretation is true? The answer is, I admit, a weak one, though I know none better. An interpretation is true for you if it registers with you as being true. Even those moments where a new insight is granted must be validated by your experience. "There is no dream without nonsense," say the rabbis.[55] There is no interpretation without nonsense as well. The best you can do is keep an open mind, looking for insights that speak to your circumstance.

Because it is you and your situation that determine the relevance and message of your dream, old dreams can suddenly come alive with new insight. Don't assume that just because you dreamed a dream months or even years ago that it can no longer speak to you. It may do so in a new and even more powerful way. Review your dream journal periodically—on your birthday, for example—and see if you do not find in the wild imagery of your dreams a compass for your life.

Dreams can also be used in a more directive fashion. It is traditional in Judaism to write down a question or problem with which you are wrestling. Read what you have written just before going to bed, then place the question or problem under your pillow and sleep on it. Ask your unconscious to help you resolve the issue. Upon waking, note your dreams (if any are recollected) and see how they relate to the question or problem written down the night before. The messages you receive arise from a part of yourself not always accessible to the waking mind. This is not magic, but it can work wonders.

There is knowledge open to you that reason cannot grasp. The rational mind is a great tool, but it is not the only one you have been given. The soul, or intuitive mind, also provides insights necessary for living well and wisely. The intuitive mind is a complementary tool, and it is this faculty that you exercise with pitron chalomot. The more you use dream interpretation to stimulate your intuitive thinking about things, the easier it is for your soul to communicate with you through dreams.

ECO-KASHRUT
Ethical Consumption

In Judaism, matter matters. You are obligated to treat all things, animate and inanimate, sentient and nonsentient, as manifestations of God. You must not cause unnecessary suffering to animals[56] or wantonly destroy nature.[57] You are required to protect trees and see to the health of the earth's bounty. As God says to Adam: "If you do not maintain My world, there is no one after you to set things right."[58] *Eco-kashrut* is the practice of maintaining God's world.

Traditionally *kashrut,* which means "fit," is concerned primarily with the food you eat, limiting your diet to those foods deemed proper by the Torah and her commentators. Eco-kashrut, or ethical consumption, extends this concern to all consumables. Nevertheless, it, too, limits what you can eat, upholding Torah's ideal of vegetarianism as the ideal diet.

I give you every seed-bearing plant that is upon the earth and every tree that has seed-bearing fruit: they shall be yours for food.[59]

Rashi (1040–1105), perhaps the most famous Torah commentator, taught:

God did not permit Adam and his wife to kill a creature and to eat its flesh. Only green herbs should they all eat together.[60]

Other major commentators, such as Ibn Ezra (1092–1167), Maimonides, and Nachmanides (1194–1270), all agreed. Even among more modern Torah commentators Rashi is upheld. Moses Cassuto (1883–1951), for example, taught that Torah permits people to use animals for the services they can provide, but does not permit them to be used for food.

Vegetarianism is not simply a dietary ideal. It is a practice designed to enhance your capacity for compassion. The Jewish philosopher Joseph Albo (died 1444) argued that vegetarianism would curb the human potential for violence. If we are forbidden to shed the blood of an animal, how much more are we forbidden to shed the blood of a fellow human being.

Torah envisions a vegetarian universe:

And to every beast of the earth, and to every fowl of the air, and to everything that creeps upon the earth,

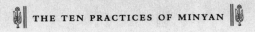

wherein there is a living soul, I have given green herbs for food.[61]

In this world

> the wolf shall dwell with the lamb; the leopard lie down with the kid; and the lion, like the ox, shall eat straw . . .[62]

and earthlings (*adam*) maintain the earth (*adamah*).[63]

If Torah envisions a vegetarian universe, why does Judaism allow the slaughtering and eating of animals for food? Rav Abraham Isaac Hacohen Kook (1865–1935), the first chief rabbi of pre-state Israel, held that vegetarianism was the spiritual ideal of God and Torah for all time. It cannot be, taught Rav Kook, that God, who created all living things, and who established vegetarianism as the natural diet for both human beings and animals, would, over the course of time, come to discover that vegetarianism was wrong. There had to be another explanation for the human penchant for meat.

The Polish sage Isaac Hebensteit provided that explanation when he wrote in 1929 that God did not want people to eat meat but allowed it conditionally, given the inability of the earth to produce grains, fruits, and vegetables after the Flood in the time of Noah. Unfortunately once the taste for meat was acquired it was impossible to return to vegetarianism. The ideal, however, was never abandoned. In fact, Rabbi Hebensteit taught, the Torah's prohibition against consuming the blood of an animal was imposed specifically to remind people that eating meat was a concession to human taste, not an ideal human diet.

It isn't only in pre-Flood times that we find God urging the people toward vegetarianism. While the Hebrews wandered in the wilderness of Sinai, God met their dietary needs with manna. The people complained, however, and demanded meat to eat. God was angry with them for this but supplied the meat nonetheless. Yet even as the Hebrews ate the meat a plague broke out among them, killing many.[64]

This story makes at least two points regarding diet. First, God tried to lead the people back to vegetarianism through a diet of manna. Second, when people did eat meat it resulted in illness. Torah made sure that meat eating would be forever linked to sickness and death, and the story would act as a warning about the right diet God demands. The place in which the story occurred is called "the Graves of Lust," alluding to the fact that it was the people's lust for meat that resulted in so many deaths. Manna sustained them in good health for forty years; meat killed them midmeal.

When the Hebrews were instructed in how to live in the Holy Land, a meatless diet again played a crucial role.

> For the Lord your God brings you into a good land,
> a land of streams and springs and fountains flowing forth
> in valleys and hills; a land of wheat and barley, of vines
> and fig trees and pomegranates, a land of olive trees and

honey; a land in which you shall eat bread without scarcity, you shall lack for nothing therein. . . . And you shall eat and be satisfied, and bless the Lord your God for the good land which God has given you.[65]

When the Jews were exiled from their land and their prophets dreamed of return, they continued to envision a land in which the inhabitants ate no meat:

> I shall return my people from captivity, and they shall rebuild the ruined cities and inhabit them, and they shall plant vineyards and drink the wine from them, and they shall make gardens and eat the fruit from them, and I shall plant them upon their land.[66]

Vegetarianism is central to holy living as Judaism has understood it for thousands of years. Even when allowing for the eating of meat, traditional Judaism made the practice so difficult that the actual consumption of meat was, until modern times, quite rare.

Eco-kashrut continues the ancient ideal of eating a vegetarian diet. Eco-kashrut is not an all-or-nothing practice. You can place yourself on the spectrum of eco-kashrut by taking even small steps toward minimizing your meat consumption. You may choose to start, if you haven't already, by avoiding all pork products and shellfish. From there you might proceed to limiting your meat eating to Shabbat and restricting the meat you do eat to kosher-slaughtered meat. Some followers of Minyan take a further step and eat only organically grown animals. Ultimately, of course, you hope to eliminate the eating of meat altogether.

I myself have not yet reached the Torah's vegan ideal. While I have refrained from eating meat for years, I do continue to eat fish. When challenged to take the next step, I humbly borrow from Franz Rosenzweig, who was once asked if he prayed with tefillin (phylacteries) and replied: "Not yet." Rosenzweig did not reject the importance of tefillin, he only admitted to not being ready to take on that discipline. In the future, who knows. I feel the same about fish.

There is more to eco-kashrut than simply diet. The act of eating, too, becomes an opportunity for ethical reflection and spiritual insight.

Rabbi Arthur Waskow calls attention to a marvelous passage of Torah: "They saw God, and they ate and drank."[67] Drawing upon earlier Hasidic commentary, Waskow sees this text as urging you to see God in your food. Seeing God in your food means that you are aware of what Waskow calls the "great web of life."

The next time you sit down to eat, pause for a moment, and consider what lies before you. That slice of bread was once a grain of wheat. To become something more, it had to interact with soil, rain, the sun, the seasons. And these, in turn, depend upon even larger systems, leading us not only to the planet as a whole, but to the entire universe of which that planet is but a small part. If even the most distant planet in our solar system were not present for this grain, neither it nor you could exist.

Yet even the vast array of nature is not sufficient to bring you that slice of bread. Someone has to plant the seed and harvest it; thresh the wheat and process it. It has to be shipped, baked, packaged, and sold. That single slice of bread contains in a very real way the entire enterprise of life, and you are about to consume it in order to further that enterprise through your own life. Being aware of this, how can you not see God when you sit down to eat and drink? And, seeing God, how can you not give thanks and utter blessings of praise?

Before you eat, close your eyes and offer a brief prayer of thanksgiving. When you open your eyes take a moment to appreciate the colors and textures of what you are about to eat. Food should delight the senses, and the more aware you are of the joy of eating, the less you actually consume, finding yourself satisfied with a little eaten with awareness rather than a lot gobbled up thoughtlessly.

Here are the traditional blessings before a meal:

Baruch Ata Adonai Eloheinu Melech ha-olam
- *ha-motzi lechem min ha-aretz* (over grain)
- *borai pri ha-adamah* (over vegetables)
- *borai pri ha-etz* (over fruit)
- *borai pri ha-gaphen* (over wine)

These translate as "Blessed is the Source of Life, the Fountain of Being, by whose power the earth gives birth to grain [vegetables, fruit, the vine]."

In addition to the traditional Hebrew blessing, you might choose to say something like the following:

> May I live in a manner worthy of the gift of this food. May I turn from ingratitude to gratitude, and eat only what I need. May I use this food for the realization of the way of wisdom, service, and loving kindness.

When you finish eating, offer a prayer of appreciation and affirmation:

> May the food I have just eaten find honor by sustaining me in my quest for holiness.

Food is not the only concern of eco-kashrut. Everything you consume should comply with the highest ethical standards, and you should take into consideration the environmental impact of what you use and purchase to determine whether or not it is proper, fit, and kosher. Eco-kashrut is linked directly with environmentalism.

Eco-kashrut's environmental concerns are as old as Torah:

> When you besiege a city a long time in order to capture it, you must not destroy its trees, wielding the ax against them. You may eat of them, but you must not cut them down. Are trees of the field human that they might

retreat before you into the city? Only trees which you know do not yield food may be destroyed....[68]

From this concern the rabbis derived four general principles. Followers of Minyan are urged to take each of these seriously and to apply them in their everyday life.

The first is the Principle Against Waste. You must take care to waste nothing. Thus the Talmud teaches that you must adjust an oil lamp so that it does not burn too quickly and waste fuel.[69] Certainly today this would apply to all manner of fuel usage. Turn off lights when they are not needed, and make the effort to use bulbs that are more fuel-efficient. Take care not to overheat or overcool your home, school, or office. Keep your car in top condition to minimize its negative effect on the environment. Recycle cans, glass, and paper goods.

The second is the Principle Against Unnecessary Destruction. If something must be destroyed, take care not to destroy more than is necessary. For example, the Talmudic sage Rav Huna wanted to test his son's temper and tore a silk purse in front of him. The rabbis challenged his choice of methods, claiming that it involved the needless destruction of an object. Rav Huna defended himself by showing them that he deliberately tore the purse along a seam so that it could be resewn.[70]

When dealing with this principle in a Minyan workshop, I ask participants to take a mental inventory of the use of paper goods in their homes. Do you use paper towels when a sponge would do just as well? Do you use multi-ply toilet tissue the same way you might single-ply—that is, balling it up and thus using more than is needed? Do you use napkins when a facial tissue is more appropriate? Do you use paper napkins when cloth might be more environmentally sound? I don't mean to be picky about all of this. I am only suggesting ways in which you can begin to apply this principle at home.

The third is the Principle Against Spoiling Food. Food has to be handled in such a manner as to protect its freshness. You are forbidden to allow good food to spoil deliberately. Thus the sages ruled that you should not toss bread from one person to another, lest it fall and become inedible. Nor when handing food to people should you pass liquids over bread, lest it spill and ruin the bread.[71]

This principle led members of one Minyan retreat to negotiate with a local supermarket to rescue foodstuffs tossed into their Dumpsters at the close of each business day. They created a system for collecting the food and transporting it to a local community food bank and soup kitchen.

How can you begin to reduce spoilage at home? Do you tend to prepare far more food than is consumed at a meal? Are leftovers eaten or allowed to spoil in the refrigerator? Do you compost?

The fourth is the Principle of Respect. There are three aspects of this principle: respect for your body, respect for nature, and respect for animals. With regard to the body, you are obligated to maintain proper hygiene, diet, and exercise; to strive toward eating a vegetarian diet; and to consume nothing that is harmful to you.

Regarding respect for nature, you must consume nothing that causes harm to other beings or the planet; you are asked not to invest in companies that harm the earth or earthlings; you are challenged to minimize the negative impact your life has on the planet. For example, don't let the tap water run while brushing your teeth or shaving; place a brick in your toilet tank to reduce the amount of water used each time you flush; minimize the use of air-conditioning.

Regarding respect for animals, you must do your best not to cause them needless suffering. Eco-kashrut prohibits wearing animal fur and urges you not to purchase personal hygiene products that involve animal testing. In a more proactive vein, living by the principles of eco-kashrut might lead you to adopt a pet from the local pound; to support your local ASPCA; and, of course, to move toward becoming a vegetarian.

My suggestions are in no way comprehensive. They are meant only to encourage you to look for ways to apply the practice of eco-kashrut in your life. Spiritual practice is not only about meditation and mystical awakening, it is about caring for the world as a manifestation of God.

TESHUVAH
Self-Perfection

Teshuvah, from the Hebrew word shuv, "to turn," is traditionally translated as "repentance." There are four stages to repentance: admitting past wrongdoing, feeling genuine remorse, refraining from that action in the future, and channeling your energies into doing good. In the process of accomplishing these four stages, you create for yourself a new persona, or, as the Bible puts it, you make for yourself "a new heart."[72]

Teshuvah implies action. Just as you chose to do a wrongful act, so you can choose to right the wrong in the present and do good in the future. It is always within your power to return your steps to the right path.

The rabbis took this notion of turning very seriously. It is central to their understanding of human free will. Because you have the power to turn, to perfect yourself, you are never simply a creature of habit. You choose how you act moment to moment. Indeed, according to the rabbis, the power to turn from evil preceded the very creation of the world. Before evil existed, God had already established the power to turn from it and do good.[73]

Teshuvah, however, is not just a matter of willpower. We all know how hard it is to do the right thing, even when we are clear as to what that is. Judaism teaches that all we have to do is make the first move; if we turn toward righteousness, the power of God will come to our aid and help us complete the process.

God says to Israel: My children, open for Me an aperture of repentance as narrow as the eye of a needle, and I will open for you gates through which wagons and coaches can pass.[74]

The sages were not naive in their assessment of repentance, however. They struggled to understand how a past deed might be righted when the hurt caused by that deed could not be undone. In the end they had no answer for this, but instead relied upon the grace of God.

> They asked of Wisdom: What is the punishment of sinners? Wisdom replied: Evil pursues sinners (Proverbs 13:21). They asked of Prophecy: What is the punishment of sinners? Prophecy replied: The soul that sins shall die (Ezekiel 18:4). They asked of the Holy One, blessed be He: What is the punishment of sinners? And God replied: Let them repent and they will find atonement."[75]

So sure were the rabbis of God's compassion, they taught that even those who have done evil all their lives, if they sincerely repented at the moment of death, they, too, would be pardoned.[76] From this the Talmudic sage Rabbi Eliezer derived the following teaching:

> Repent one day before you die.
> His disciples asked him: Do we know, then, on what day we will die?
> Rabbi Eliezer replied: All the more reason to repent today, lest you die tomorrow.[77]

Teshuvah does not remove the desire to do hurtful things. As long as we live we struggle with our dual nature of

Yetzer ha-Tov and Yetzer ha-Rah, the inclination to do good and the inclination to do evil. Teshuvah simply encourages us to make a habit out of being better.

Sa'adiah Gaon (882–942), an Egyptian Jew who became the leading Jewish philosopher of the tenth century, offered his own take on repentance. First, you must experience regret and remorse over the act. Second, you must admit to the act and renounce it as wrong. Third, you must request forgiveness from those you have wronged. Fourth, you must refrain from repeating the action in the future.

Sa'adiah also saw different levels of repentance. The highest level of teshuvah is repenting immediately after an act is committed. The damage of your action is evident to you in the immediacy of what you have done, and you are overwhelmed with remorse. You stop the action and quickly make amends. A less effective act of repentance occurs when you are confronted with punishment or disaster resulting from your action. While this may be heartfelt, it is also self-serving. The lowest category of repentance is repenting on one's deathbed. Here it is fear of retribution in an afterlife rather than a desire to set things right in this life that motivates you to repent. Sa'adiah is stricter than the Talmudic sages who upheld the praiseworthy nature of deathbed teshuvah.

A century after Sa'adiah, Bahya Ibn Paquda, a Jewish philosopher living in Muslim Spain, made teshuvah a central element of his attempt to reinvigorate Jewish spirituality. Little is known of this eleventh-century sage, but his book *Duties of the*

Heart continues to be a central text for traditional Jews. Bahya wrote the book to offset the legal focus of the rabbis of his time. In addition to following the duties of the body, the ritual and legal obligations to which the Jew is obligated, Bahya taught that there are equally essential duties of the heart: spiritual obligations that, if followed, can lead to the perfection of the human being.

According to Bahya, there are seven stages of repentance. First, you must be convinced that you are responsible for the action in question. Second, you must realize that the act was a wrongful one. Third, you must become aware that there is a consequence to your action. Fourth, you must understand that your deed is not being ignored; even if no one else knows what you have done, you know and so does God. Fifth, you must realize that repentance alone will return you to the path of righteousness. Sixth, you must realize that the joy you received from doing the wrong thing is not as great as the joy you will receive from doing the right thing. Seventh, you must sincerely resolve to break with the habits of evil to which you have grown accustomed.

The popularity of Bahya's teaching and the centrality of teshuvah in Jewish thought continued into modern times. Yet it was in the modern period that the notion of teshuvah began to change. Whereas for centuries teshuvah meant returning to ethical behavior, in the modern period it took on the added and ever more dominant meaning of returning to tradition and religious ritual.

Central to this shift is the life and work of the German Jewish philosopher Franz Rosenzweig (1886–1929). Rosenzweig grew up in an assimilated household and was drawn more and more strongly to the teachings of Christianity. In 1913 he decided to convert to Christianity. Recognizing the Jewish origins of his newly chosen faith, Rosenzweig decided to immerse himself in Jewish living in order to enrich his Christianity. During a Yom Kippur service at a small Orthodox synagogue in Berlin just prior to his formal conversion to Christianity, Rosenzweig underwent a profound spiritual transformation. While never writing down what he experienced, from that day on he devoted himself to learning, living, and teaching traditional Judaism. Under Rosenzweig's influence teshuvah no longer meant turning from evil and doing good, it meant turning from assimilationist thinking and embracing the traditions of Judaism.

In the context of Minyan, however, teshuvah retains its original meaning as turning from evil and doing good. It refers to your ability to learn from life in order to perfect your living. No one is perfect, yet everyone is perfectible. Being perfectible means that you can do a little better today than you did yesterday. In order to help you with this, the Satmar rebbe, Rabbi Moshe Teitelbaum (born 1915), advises you to take an accounting of your day just before you go to sleep. You should note all your good deeds, confess all your bad deeds, and make a sincere promise to do better the next day: adding to the list of good deeds and subtracting from the list of bad ones.

Teshuvah is the practice of admitting your mistakes learning from them, correcting them, and not repeating them. You will always make mistakes. Teshuvah is about not making the same mistake twice.

You should observe all of your actions and watch over all of your ways so as not to leave yourself with a bad habit or bad trait, let alone a sin or a crime. . . . Carefully examine your ways and weigh them daily. . . . You should set aside definite times and hours for this weighing so that it is not a fortuitous matter, but one which is conducted with the greatest regularity.[78]

Among the many actions the sages urge us to watch, speech holds a place of great importance, especially hurtful speech, or *lashon harah*. According to the rabbis, speaking ill or falsely of others is the most common error we fall into. If we are to move ourselves toward perfection, we must start with correcting our speech.

There is a Hasidic story about a town gossip. This fellow thoughtlessly told and retold stories about others that brought them shame. The town's rabbi met with the man and confronted him with his words. The man was stunned. He had no idea he was spreading such hurt. He broke into tears and begged the rabbi for help: "There must be something I can do to atone for the wickedness I have done."

The rabbi instructed the man to take four pillows out into a field. Once there he was to slice open each pillow with a knife and shake its feathers into the wind. The man thanked the rabbi and rushed off to do as he was told. He purchased four fine feather pillows and cut them open in the field, watching as the feathers scattered in every direction.

He returned to the rabbi to let him know he had completed his penance. "Not quite," said the rabbi. "Now go back to the field and retrieve the feathers."

"But that is impossible," said the man. "The winds have taken them everywhere."

"It is the same with your words," the rabbi said gravely. "Just as you cannot retrieve the feathers once spilled, so you cannot withdraw words once spoken. No matter how sincerely you desire to undo what you have done, the harm caused by thoughtless speech cannot be rectified."

The Jewish concern with speech begins with the Torah: "Do not go about as a gossip among your people."[79] From this injunction the sages derived the teaching that you should avoid saying anything negative about people, even if true, unless there is a compelling and legitimate reason for doing so.

When you were little you learned "Sticks and stones may break my bones, but words will never hurt me." A Jewish version of this would be "Sticks and stones may break my bones, but my body knows how to heal; words alone can carry a hurt I will forever feel." Recognizing the power of words to cause needless pain is central to the practice of teshuvah, self-perfection.

According to the sages there are three categories of hurtful speech.

The first is everyday gossip. This refers to the all-too-common habit of talking about other people behind their backs. Gossip should be avoided even if it appears to be positive. The longer you talk about someone, even if at first you are talking about the good that someone did, the more likely it is that you will begin to criticize. It is human nature to be drawn to the negative in other people.

How many times have you heard something like the following: "Martha is a wonderful person. I can't begin to tell all the great things she has done for me over the years. Of course, she does have her faults. Take last Friday, for example. You won't believe this, but Martha actually . . ."

When saying something positive about someone, make sure to stop once the compliment is given.

The second category of hurtful speech is making negative or derogatory remarks about people that might cause physical, psychological, or financial harm. You should avoid this kind of speech even if the remarks are true.

A man once came into my office to show me an ancient coin he had recently purchased during a trip to Israel. He was so proud of his find and of his skill at negotiating a low price for the coin. I looked at the coin and recognized it as indeed being old, but also, given its condition, being anything but valuable. The man had greatly overpaid for the coin. Yet I said none of this. What good would it have done? In fact, a negative comment from me, even if couched in a joke, would have caused him unnecessary sadness.

I could have told him he had been the victim of exorbitant overpricing, but the purchase had already been made. If he had come to me beforehand and asked for my opinion, then I would have been free to suggest other dealers. In this case I simply expressed genuine joy at his happiness over his coin and talked with him about the historical period from which it came. I also said that if he was interested in purchasing other artifacts, I could put him in touch with some of Israel's most qualified dealers. He left happy and supported.

Avoiding hurtful speech in this way often riles those who love to introduce their tales with "I have to be honest. . . ." What such people really mean is that they can excuse their hurtful speech by hiding behind a curtain of honesty, but honesty never excuses nastiness.

The rabbis ask: What if you attend a wedding and are asked to compliment the bride, whom you find to be anything but attractive? Do you say, "Well, I have to be honest, you really look horrible"? Of course not. Your obligation is to be kind while not lying. So, the sages suggest, say this: "You never looked more radiant." Or this: "Your happiness fills the entire room."

The only exception to this is when you have information about a person that another needs to know for his or her own protection. For example, a friend is about to marry a man you know to be already married. Or you are asked for a job reference for someone you know to be untrustworthy. Or you are talking with a person about to enter into a business arrangement with someone whom you know to be a con artist. If you are absolutely sure of the facts, and the sharing of the information is clearly in the interest of protecting another from fraud or abuse, then you are required to share the information.

The third category is the spreading of falsehood. Most people do not go around deliberately denigrating others. Yet most of us have on occasion passed on rumors that proved to be untrue. This is a violation of the prohibition against hurtful speech. Stereotyping people and groups falls into this category as well.

During Minyan retreats people often object to making speech such an important part of spiritual practice. After all, they say, we tend to talk without thinking. This is exactly the point. Words are important. Words can make or break a person. If you talk without thinking, you will say things you will regret. But regret isn't enough. You cannot undo the damage gossip and hurtful speech can wreak. The key to teshuvah regarding your speech is this: "When you speak to your fellow man, let your intention be to speak with your Creator."[80] In other words, recognize and live up to the divine potential in yourself and in everyone with whom you speak.

When people are speaking about love, for example, you should turn your mind to the love of God, and think about how you should love only God. Or when the talk is about wealth, you should think that it is from God that wealth comes, and so also honor. And do the same when the conversation is about anything relating to beauty, splendor, or glory. So, too, when the talk is about worldly fears, think that you should fear only God. And so all other things. You should attend to what is before you, and

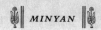

as a result you will never cease from God-consciousness, even when you are conversing with other people.[81]

Look for opportunities to help and support the person with whom you are speaking. Look for the greater meaning in the conversation. The Hasidim believe that everything that happens to you happens in order to teach you something about your own life and how you are to improve it. Nothing is without ethical import to one who chooses to see everything as a lesson. The Baal Shem Tov applies this idea even to the indiscretions and errors of others. Rather than judge others, you are to use their mistakes to remind you of your own.

If you see another person doing something ugly, recognize that same ugliness in yourself. Know that God has mercifully brought this sight before your eyes to remind you of that fault in yourself, so as to bring you an opportunity for teshuvah.

If you see someone violating the Sabbath, or desecrating God's name some other way, you should examine your own deeds and you will certainly find among them similar failings.

Or if you hear profanity or obscene language, you should consider the quality of your own speech, and recall moments when you failed to conduct yourself modestly. . . .

All who follow this path and behave in this way will

judge others favorably . . . for they will realize that they are no better than the other person, sharing the same faults and blemishes. And they will repent completely for all the things that they have done wrong. . . .

For there is nothing that happens in this world without a purpose, and everything you experience was sent to you from heaven for you to see and from which to learn . . . there is not even a word spoken in their presence in which they cannot hear some hint from heaven to remind them of some forgotten error. . . .[82]

Teshuvah, turning from your mistakes and moving in the direction of perfection, allows you to learn from everyone and everything without condemnation. Not that you excuse the wrongs of others, but you do not use them to elevate or excuse yourself.

Here are some guidelines for practicing teshuvah through right speech. When speaking with other people, begin and end your conversation with shalom, "peace." This is the natural way of speaking in Hebrew. Surrounding your words with "peace" will help remind you to use your words to promote peace.

Listen to yourself while you talk. Allow a part of yourself to observe dispassionately what you are saying as you are saying it. As soon as you hear yourself speaking falsely or hurtfully, stop, apologize for having gotten carried away, and begin again more carefully.

Set aside time each week to reflect on the quality of your

conversation. Review some of the conversations you have had during the week and ask yourself how you might have handled things better. Take note of what things trigger you to anger or gossip. The more aware you are of these triggers, the more control you have over how you respond to them.

Maintain the preciousness of speech by setting for yourself a "word fast," a day when you refrain from talking altogether. Use this time to evaluate the power of words and commit yourself to improving the quality of your speech. If a word fast seems too severe, set a day for fasting from lies. Pick one day a month during which you will weigh each word you speak and take extreme care to say nothing that you do not know to be positively true. Of course, don't allow truth to excuse nastiness. Be honest and compassionate.

You can begin your general practice of teshuvah through right speech by setting aside fifteen minutes each day during which you will take special care not to gossip or use hurtful speech. Choose a time that is usually given over to such speech: lunchtime with friends or break time over coffee, for example. Slowly increase the amount of time you devote to this practice.

This exercise has great staying power: your consciousness is raised regarding the quality of your speech, and you will find your speech improved throughout the day. Even when you are not formally practicing teshuvah you will find yourself sensitized to the words you use and the way you use them. You will become more aware of the impact your words have on others and on yourself, and you will naturally curb your tongue.

Teshuvah is a learning experience. It requires you to pay close attention to what you do and how you do it. Set aside time just before bed to review your day and see what you can learn from it. Ask yourself these questions to help focus on ethical perfection:

- How was I better today than yesterday?
- What mistakes did I make today?
- What can I learn from these mistakes?
- What can I do tomorrow to make amends?
- What must I do never to repeat these mistakes?
- What was the quality of my speech today?
- What harm did my words cause?
- What can I do tomorrow to make my speech more thoughtful?

Keep a journal of your responses to these questions. Make a list of traits you would like to eliminate from your behavior. Make a complementary list of traits you would like to add to your behavior. Refer to these lists each morning, picking one trait to avoid and one to practice each day. In time your journal should reflect real changes in your action that reflect real growth in your character.

SHABBAT
Sabbath

Shabbat is about recognizing the importance of rest and renewal in the midst of the harrowing and hectic life you lead by setting aside one day a week, from sunset Friday to just after sunset Saturday, to open yourself to reflection and renewal. This is the purpose of Shabbat, and it is the purpose, as opposed to the traditional obligations and restrictions, with which Minyan is primarily concerned.

The idea of punctuating the relentlessness of labor with formal times of rest was first introduced to the world through the Torah. The earliest biblical reference to a seventh day of rest comes from the book of Genesis.

> Heaven and earth, and all their components, were completed. With the seventh day, God finished all the work that He had done. God ceased on the seventh day from all the work that He had been doing. God blessed the seventh day, and declared it holy, for it was on this day that God ceased from all the work that He had been creating. . . .[83]

This passage in itself makes no reference to a fixed day of rest or a formal Sabbath, nor does it obligate anyone else to observe it. This is God's day off. Yet it is here that we learn something very important about Shabbat: it is built into the very structure of creation.

The whole isn't finished until God introduces the seventh day, the day of cessation. Did the ancients imagine that God gets tired? Did they project onto their image of God their own desire for a few hours' rest? Or did they discover through their own lives the fundamental place rest and renewal have in a world dependent upon work?

The authors who shaped the Creation story lived in a world of ceaseless labor. Yet they saw the need for balancing work with rest. They knew that the world works best when it doesn't work all the time. So in their telling of Creation they did something very revolutionary: not only did they hallow work by having it come directly from God as a deliberate expression of God, but they hallowed rest by having God rest.

God's seventh day is holy. It is different from the other six, yet it is not better than them. Genesis does not suggest a laborless ideal. Labor is sanctified every time God looks at creation and says, "It is good." What the ancients saw, and what their descendants sought to institutionalize, was the fundamental need everything has for cessation, nondoing, and renewal. Creation isn't complete until there is a time when nothing needs to be done.

In the first presentation of the Ten Commandments the connection is made between God resting on the seventh day of Creation and you and I resting on the seventh day of the week.

Remember the Sabbath day to keep it holy. You can work during the six weekdays and do all your tasks. But the seventh day is the Sabbath to God your Lord. Do not do anything that constitutes work. [This applies to] you, your son, your daughter, your slave, your maid, your animal, and the foreigner in your gates. It was during the six weekdays that God made the heaven, the earth, the sea, and all that is in them, but he rested on the seventh day. God therefore blessed the Sabbath day and made it holy.[84]

No longer is rest the privilege of the rich, but all of us must rest one day a week. To make the point crystal clear the Bible specifies that children are free on this day, that slaves cannot be made to work on this day, that strangers who just happen to be sojourning in your town or staying in your home cannot be asked to work on this day. What was the privilege of the elite becomes the universal right of all; even animals are free from labor on this day.

As Jewish civilization develops, the Shabbat ideal extends its reach beyond sentient beings to embrace all creation. Every seven years the earth itself is to rest. For twelve months no field is to be plowed, no crop harvested. The earth has her Sabbath, too. Every seventh cycle of seven years knows another level of Sabbath rest as civilization itself lies fallow. This Jubilee Year is one in which the original equality between people is reinstated and the haves and have-nots are equalized. The quest for riches is not allowed to continue indefinitely. Every fiftieth year we gather together, divide the world's wealth evenly, and begin the process again.

It is important to your appreciation of Shabbat and your own personal commitment to making Shabbat, to realize how revolutionary this idea was. The biblical Shabbat has no known parallel in the ancient world. The Sumerian, Babylonian, and

Mesopotamian peoples all used seven as a magical number. The Mesopotamian lunar calendar, however, marks the sevens associated with the phases of the moon (the seventh, fourteenth, twenty-first, and twenty-eighth days of the month) as dangerous and unlucky. People were advised to stay home and minimize their activities on these days. This is a reverse image of the Jewish Shabbat, which sees the seventh day of the week as especially blessed and prohibits activities so as to focus on deeper issues than the workweek allows. The fear and dread associated with the series of sevens in the Mesopotamian calendar are transformed by Judaism, and Shabbat is observed as an expression of holiness.

Unlike the other seventh days in neighboring cultures, the biblical Shabbat is not tied to a celestial pattern. The seventh day is not determined by the waxing and waning of the moon or by any solar cycle. Shabbat is an independent reality tied solely to the creation of the world by God. Shabbat is world-transcending and therefore potentially world-transforming, enlarging our perspective of what life is so that we return to the workweek with a renewed vision of what life can be.

Given the total lack of precedence for Shabbat, the ancients had to link the idea of Shabbat with the highest values of the people if they were to ensure the fulfillment of its potential. Thus the Torah goes to great lengths to guarantee Shabbat a central place in the lives of those who take the Bible seriously:

> Keep My Sabbaths as a sign between Me and you for
> all generations, realizing that through it I, God, am mak-

ing you holy. Protect the sacredness of this day. Anyone doing work [on the Sabbath] shall be cut off from the people. Anyone violating it shall be put to death. Six days you may work, but keep the seventh as a Sabbath, holy to God. Whoever does any work on this day shall be put to death. The Israelites shall thus make the Sabbath an eternal covenant. It is a sign between Me and the Israelites that in six days God made heaven and earth, and on the seventh, He ceased working and was refreshed.[85]

Between the positive reinforcement of Shabbat as divine covenant and the negative reinforcement of capital punishment, the authors of the Torah could be fairly certain that Shabbat would be taken seriously. Yet how many of us make Shabbat?

We who are perpetually tired, run-down, and on the verge of exhaustion seem unable to take even one day each week to catch our breath. You would think that now more than ever the idea of Shabbat would be a winning one. Yet it isn't. Why?

My guess is that for most of us the meaning of Shabbat is lost amid the details of Sabbath law. Take, for example, listening to the stereo on Shabbat.

I personally find great spiritual uplift in spending Sabbath time listening to classical music, and I do so almost weekly. Yet this actually violates the Sabbath law against lighting a fire on Shabbat.

The Torah prohibits the kindling of fire on Shabbat for good reason. In ancient times fire was the main engine of so much work that to allow people to kindle a fire and yet not allow them to use it for some constructive bit of commerce was to ask for the impossible. The temptation would be too great. The Torah eliminates the temptation by prohibiting lighting the fire.

I can understand and appreciate this in the context of history. It is the equivalent of my not turning on my computer on Shabbat even to play a game with my son. I do most of my work on my computer, and the temptation to finish my latest essay would be too much. Why tempt myself? No computers on the Sabbath makes it easier for me not to work on the Sabbath. And not working allows me to focus on the real intent of Shabbat: rest and renewal.

But should this also extend to my stereo? According to Sabbath law, I cannot turn on my stereo because in the process of doing so, I am making an electrical connection, which violates the law against kindling a fire on Shabbat. I could leave my stereo on all night Friday and all day Saturday, taking care to turn it on before the Sabbath. Then I would not be violating the law and could listen to music. But doing so seems like a terrible waste of energy, which violates my concern for eco-kashrut. It also leaves me with the uncomfortable feeling that Shabbat is somehow a game for lawyers. The idea shifts from focusing on the intent to finding the loophole in the law that will allow me to do what I want. I find this so blatantly silly that at times I am tempted to dispense with the Sabbath altogether.

Rather than do that, I choose to free myself from the law and return to the intent: setting aside one day a week for rest and spiritual renewal. I make the purpose of Shabbat rather than the laws associated with it my guiding principle when deciding what is and what is not allowable. If you find the rabbinical traditions of Shabbat meaningful and helpful to you, then by all means use them. But if they are not, do not let them keep you from observing Shabbat in your own way.

The ultimate guide to your making Shabbat should be your understanding of the rabbinic teaching that Shabbat is a foretaste of the world-to-come. On Shabbat you practice living in the world-to-come, the world where the division between spiritual and physical is erased and you see the holiness of all things. On Shabbat you create a world where the interdependence of matter and spirit, person and person, and person and planet is acknowledged and honored. On Shabbat you act as if there were nothing to change, no need for willfulness or desire. On Shabbat you act as if everything lived out its potential, doing what needs to be done with effortless grace and compassion.

On Shabbat you live as if you were spiritually awake and aware. What a phenomenal idea! How do you know what spiritual awakening is like? Make Shabbat. How do you know what spiritual living is like? Make Shabbat. Live for one day as if you were at home in the universe. Live for one day without trying to control the people around you and the situations in which you find yourself. Live for one day in a state of total acceptance.

Do you grasp the wonder and challenge of this day? Not a day without desire; that is not possible. But a day not to act on those desires.

The Sabbath is a day set aside to live as if you did not desire the world to conform to your wishes. You don't have to be free of desire, you only have to live as if you were free. This is why the rabbis called the Sabbath a foretaste of the world-to-come. In the world-to-come, awake to the holiness of all things as expressions of God, and you will not seek to impose your will. On Shabbat you practice living this way and taste what is in store for you.

I never understood the real importance of this "living as if" aspect of Shabbat until a friend of mine, Professor Nathan Katz of Florida International University's Department of Judaic Studies, told me of a visit he and a group of rabbis from the United States made to the Dalai Lama in Dharamsala.

During a conversation between the Dalai Lama and Rabbi Zalman Schachter-Shalomi, the rabbi explained the idea of Shabbat as a foretaste of the world-to-come. The Dalai Lama said there was a similar idea in Tibetan Buddhism. Monks undertake long stays in isolation during which they visualize one of the deities of the Tibetan Buddhist pantheon. The visualization becomes so intense that the deity comes alive. At this point the monks merge with the deity, seeking to take on its attributes by living as if they were the deity.

This the Dalai Lama related to Shabbat as the foretaste of the world-to-come. Like the meditating monk, he explained to the assembled scholars and sages, you Jews are visualizing the world-to-come and embodying its attributes by living Shabbat as if it were the world-to-come.

What is the attribute you embody as you model the

world-to-come through Shabbat? Freedom. The way you breathe, the way you sit, the way you spend your time—all manifest freedom from the demands of the world.

The Bible makes an explicit link between Shabbat and freedom in its second listing of the Ten Commandments. Here the importance of Shabbat is no longer that God rested on the seventh day, but that God liberated the Jews from slavery in Egypt.

> Six days you may labor to accomplish all your tasks, but the seventh day is the Sabbath to God your Lord, so do nothing that constitutes work. Neither you, your son, your daughter, your slaves and servants, your ox, your donkey, your [other] animals, nor the foreigner who is in your gates. Even your slaves and servants will then be able to rest just as you do. You must remember that you were slaves in Egypt, when God your Lord brought you out with a strong hand and an outstretched arm. It is for this reason that God your Lord has commanded you to keep the Sabbath.[86]

The Israelites' experience of slavery and their subsequent liberation from it became the foundation for their understanding of the significance and meaning of Shabbat. Shabbat is not simply a remembering of liberations past, but a catalyst for future liberations as well.

The greater liberation toward which Shabbat points is freedom from the fearsome and fearful desire to control the world and bend it to your will. "For six days shall you labor." Why? To get what you desire. To make things come out the way you want them to. To make the world conform to your will. The seventh day will be a respite from all this. A rest from desire, from conforming, from confronting, from becoming. The seventh day is a day for simply being.

Shabbat rest is a state of absolute armistice between you and your world. For twenty-five hours you refrain from bending the world to your will and live with the radical freedom that relinquishing the act of control offers.

When I was a child I learned of a rabbinic ruling that speaks directly to this notion of acceptance. It is permitted to walk your dog on the Sabbath. You can walk in the woods, play, run, lie out in the sun or under the cooling shade of a thick-leaved tree. You can thoroughly enjoy each other's company. But, when you return home, you are forbidden from brushing your dog's fur to make it nice and neat again.

What a grand message of acceptance! Go out and enjoy your dog, but do not expect her to conform to your idea of neatness. It is natural for her to get messy. It is normal for her to pick up a topcoat of pine needles. That is what happens in the woods. Relax, enjoy it, and do not attempt to make nature conform to your definition of neat. On the Sabbath you are free to explore and enjoy what is; you are not free to transform it into what you want.

How to begin your practice of Shabbat? First you have to set aside the time. Start with Friday night. Invite friends to dinner.

Light the Sabbath candles. Ask people to bring something to read aloud and discuss to help elevate conversation to serious topics of spirituality. Don't watch television. You might consider going to a synagogue for Friday evening services. Eventually you might expand your Shabbat into Saturday, attending services, studying the weekly Torah portion, reading, talking with friends and loved ones.

The details of your Shabbat are very much up to you. Keep in mind, however, that this isn't simply a day off. It is a day for reflection and renewal of your spirit. Find things to do that help you in this regard.

To help you begin the practice of Shabbat, here are a series of brief readings and rituals around the tradition of lighting the Sabbath candles on Friday evening. As your appreciation o Shabbat deepens, I urge you to explore a fuller, more traditiona Shabbat experience.

Giving Tzedakah

It is traditional to give tzedakah before making Shabbat.
As you prepare to place money in your tzedakah box,
read the following:

In love I take upon myself
the challenge of this moment
as a reminder of the purpose of creation.
In peace I take upon myself
the sanctity of this moment
as a catalyst for healing and unity.

Blessed is the Source of Life
whose creative power hallows rest and renewal.

Candlelighting

As you prepare to light two Shabbat candles,
read the following:

Darkness blankets me.
Comforting, perhaps a bit frightening.
It harbors both dreams and demons.
I tap it for solace. I delve it for options.
I flee it for fear that it mirrors
that which I wish so desperately to avoid: Me.
Yet I am here not to embrace the dark
but to kindle the light.
Not to close my eyes forever,
but to open them this once.
I dwell amidst the dark and bring forth light.
Soft, fragile, flickering light.
The only light I know. The only light I can bear.
I bring it, yet it isn't mine.
I kindle it, yet it isn't me.
I am the light-bearer only.

Where the world is dark with illness,
let me kindle the light of healing.
Where the world is bleak with suffering,

let me kindle the light of caring.
Where the world is dimmed by lies,
let me kindle the light of truth.

I vow to be worthy of this honor
as I strike this match and kindle the flame
that illumines the heart of all the world.

Baruch Ata Adonai Eloheinu Melech ha-olam asher kid'
shanu b'mitzvotav v'tzivanu l'hadleek nair shel Shabbat.

Blessed is the One beyond light and dark
by whose power I sanctify Life
with the lighting of these candles.

> *Standing in the soft glow of the Shabbat candles, read:*

> The heavens and the earth and all within them were
> finished. By the seventh day God had completed the
> work which God had been doing; and so God rested
> from all the work. Then God blessed the seventh day and
> sanctified it because on it God rested from the divine
> work of creation.[87]

You capped doing with nondoing;
You blessed becoming with being;
You honored labor and rest.
Creation was incomplete without Shabbat.

Rest reveals the importance of work.

Work reveals the importance of rest.

The two together make the world;

the two together make a human being.

I rest when I cease my struggle to control.

I rest when I abandon my pride of ownership.

I rest when I give thanks for what is.

I set aside these moments

to revel in Your work by sharing Your rest.

I set aside these moments

for mindfulness and renewal.

I set aside these moments

to review my mission and my priorities.

I set aside these moments

to honor all that I have been given.

I set aside these moments

to take stock of all that I am.

I take this time to make Sabbath;

to set aside the labors that define me

and uncover the me that cannot be defined;

to find in the quiet

friends and counselors urging me to wholeness;

to find in these hours rest and renewal;

and to open my heart to joy and my mind to truth.

May all who struggle find rest with me.

May all who suffer find solace with me.

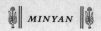

May all who hurt find healing with me.
May all who despair find purpose with me.
May all who hunger find fulfillment with me.
And may I live my life in such a way that
each moment fulfills the promise of this moment.

Before drinking the wine or grape juice:

Baruch Ata Adonai Eloheinu Melech ha-olam borai pri ha-gaphen.

Blessed is the Source of Life, the Substance of all Being,
whose creative power fashions the fruit of the vine.
May I find in this act of drinking
reminders of suffering and joy
and the humility to accept them both.

Before eating the bread:

Baruch Ata Adonai Eloheinu Melech ha-olam ha-motzi lechem min ha-aretz.

Blessed is the Source of Life, the Substance of all Being,
whose creative power brings forth grain from the earth.
May I find in this act of eating
a reminder of my obligation to both self and other.

⚗️ ‖ FELLOWSHIP ‖ ⚗️

When I first created Minyan I offered it to individuals as a private spiritual practice. While it does work that way, I quickly learned that people had a natural desire to form small communities around Minyan practice. In my own congregation a group of Minyan retreat participants created *Chavurah Saffir,* the Sapphire Fellowship. The group meets one Sunday each month to study together and support each other's efforts in each of the ten practices. In time groups like these impressed upon me the need for friends and fellowship on the spiritual path. While no one can do the work for you, it is far easier to stick with your practice when others are doing it alongside you.

Spiritual practice can be isolating. As some people move deeper into their meditation practice it is not uncommon for them to withdraw from the world around them. While there are religions that encourage this withdrawal, Judaism is not one of them. The goal of Minyan is not to remove you from the struggles of the world, but to help prepare you to meet them more effectively. The forming of community allows you to engage the world within the context of a supportive circle of friends whose freely chosen obligation is the mutual support of each other's spiritual practice and maturation.

On the simplest level, Reb Nachman of Bratzlav taught that you should have a special friend with whom to discuss matters of the spirit. Rabbi Menachem Mendel of Vitebsk (1730–

1788) said that you should speak with this friend for thirty minutes every day, sharing the mistakes you have made during the
day and helping each other to overcome them.

Finding a friend with whom to be spiritually intimate is
not easy, and you must go about doing so with caution. You need
to find a person with whom you can entrust your deepest doubts
and difficulties. You need someone who can make your spiritual
well-being a priority in his or her own life.

An acquaintance of mine placed a classified ad in a local
newspaper, seeking just such a spiritual companion. He received
over a dozen responses. Three were for dates, one was a marriage
proposal, and the rest were thoughtful letters from various Chris-
tians seeking to convert him to their faith.

Where can you find true spiritual partners?

Start with your friends. Do any of them share your interest in spirituality? Are any of them curious about religion, mysticism, or meditation? Even if they are not interested in your
particular approach to spirituality, if they are open and supportive of you and your growth (as you must be of them and theirs),
you may find them to be the perfect spiritual partners.

You can also find potential spiritual friends at various
seminars and workshops devoted to religion and spirituality.
There are many magazines available in your local bookstore that
deal with spiritual themes and advertise upcoming conferences
or other events. Investigate some of these and attend one or two
in the next year.

To mention just a few options, I suggest contacting Elat

Chayyim,[1] a Jewish spiritual retreat center, and requesting a catalog of their seminars. Write to Rabbi David Cooper at the Heart of Stillness Retreat Center[2] and ask for the dates of his meditation retreats. Write or call Rabbi Shefa Gold of the Rose Mountain Center[3] and inquire about her meditation programs. Contact the ALEPH Alliance for Jewish Renewal[4] in Philadelphia and ask about their biannual conventions. You can even call my own Rasheit Institute for Jewish Spirituality[5] and register for our fall or spring retreats.

A more challenging level of *chevruta* (fellowship) involves joining a synagogue. Many spiritually inclined Jews, however, have a hard time finding a synagogue that meets their needs: "I'm looking for a place for spiritual exploration, and instead I find cold and lifeless dens of political wrangling where ego, not God, is the true object of worship." Many synagogues are like this; many, but not all.

It is important to belong to a community. It is important to share your resources and expertise with others in the pursuit of mutually valued goals. And yes, this often involves you in communal politics. If you are serious about your spiritual practice, however, you will recognize community and synagogue to be a testing ground for your maturation. Can you maintain clarity of focus and gentleness of spirit in the face of political hassles and hostilities? It is a good measure of your spiritual development.

Explore the synagogues in your area and seek out a home among them. The best way to get a sense of what a synagogue is about is to participate in a Shabbat service, either Friday evening or Saturday morning. Notice I said "participate." Attending services and observing the scene as if on assignment for *National Geographic* will not allow you to feel the spirit the community may have to offer. Nobody feels comfortable the first time in a new environment, but do not isolate yourself in a corner. Read along with the congregation, sing or hum their songs, join in as best you can to see if indeed the fit is right.

After you return home, ask yourself how you felt. Were you uplifted, motivated, and energized by the service? Did the music move you? Was there too much or too little Hebrew? Did the rabbi's words touch you? Challenge you? Did the people look happy? Were the other congregants moved? Did they sing? Did they participate? Did they make any effort to welcome you?

If your assessment of your visit is totally negative, move on. But if not, give the synagogue a second and even a third visit. It takes time to understand what a community is trying to do and what it has to offer.

Many people expect to be welcomed by a synagogue as the long-lost prodigal child. This rarely happens. In fact, I would be wary of any group that welcomes you too quickly. If the group claims to love you without knowing you, it isn't you they love.

If you are serious about joining a particular synagogue, make time to speak with the rabbi. Learn something about her background and the kind of Judaism she espouses. Explain your desire to find a spiritual home and ask her for advice as to how you might fit into the synagogue. It helps to join and to volunteer or a committee or project that interests you. If the synagogue does nothing that excites you, chances are this is not the place for you.

If you do join, move slowly. You are the new member, and while you hope the community is open to new ideas, you cannot expect them to embrace yours without learning more about you and what you have to offer. Learn to care for others, and they may learn to care for you.

One way to make yourself more at home in a new synagogue is to bring your friends with you. You will feel more comfortable and you will have a larger voice if you join a community with others.

If the synagogue you have chosen has no spiritual *chavurah* (fellowship group) and you would like to start one, ask the rabbi how you might go about it. Some rabbis may be threatened by this, fearing a split in the congregation. Be careful to explain simply, honestly, and clearly what it is you wish to do and how you wish to do it. Be sensitive to the rabbi's feelings; he may feel slighted at the suggestion of not fulfilling your spiritual needs. Most rabbis, however, will jump at the chance to have a chavurah devoted to spiritual concerns develop within the community. In the long run this will make the entire congregation richer.

Not everyone wants or has the opportunity to join a synagogue. If you find yourself in this situation, seek out likeminded friends and start an informal chavurah of your own. Invite friends to meditate with you; to study Torah with you; to share Shabbat evening dinner with you; to celebrate Shabbat and holy days with you; to practice Minyan with you.

There is no magic formula for establishing a successful chavurah. There are a few guidelines, however. First, let people know you intend to do this. No one can read your mind. Talk it up among your friends. Congregation Beth Or in Miami began as a monthly chavurah. I placed an ad in the *Miami Herald,* inviting unaffiliated Jews to meet to discuss their spiritual needs and how we might address them together in a chavurah setting. Eighty people attended our first meeting. Twenty came back a month later to found the community formally.

Second, establish regular meetings. Start slowly. While I suggest gearing your chavurah to Shabbat observance, meeting every Shabbat may be too much at first. Begin with a once-a-month potluck Shabbat dinner. Light the candles, say the blessings over wine and challah, and eat. After dinner ask people to share their spiritual journeys or assign readings for informal discussion. Don't forget to sing. If children are involved, make a special effort to include them in dinner and candlelighting, but provide alternative programming for them during adult discussion times. Rotate responsibility for the children.

Third, explore where the chavurah would like to go. In time, a core group will emerge that is serious about maintaining your fledgling community. Talk with members about their needs and hopes for the chavurah. Begin to explore the logistics of becoming a formal community. Do you need a leader? Do you need teachers? Do you need to rent a regular place to meet? Do you need to charge dues?

Those are some things to consider, but there is much

more to establishing a successful chavurah. The people at the National Chavurah Committee[6] are a wonderfully helpful resource for both new and established communities. Contact them for guidance.

Chevruta keeps you from becoming isolated from the larger community. It is important for you to connect with others intellectually, emotionally, and spiritually. The following letter[7] from a woman I met during a Minyan retreat last summer makes the power of chevruta quite clear.

Dear Rami,

Thank you for seven marvelous days of meditation and study. Your Minyan program is a real eye-opener. I have been a Jew all my life, but I never associated Judaism with spirituality. It was always something I did because I had to. First, to please my grandparents, and then, when they had died, to honor their memory. I'm sure my parents never took any of it seriously.

Not surprisingly my synagogue experience was pretty bleak. When I found myself, in my thirties, looking to add a spiritual component to my life, the last place I thought to look was to Judaism and the synagogue. Even attending your retreat was done with some level of skepticism; my friends dragged me with them.

After studying with you, I discovered a dimension to Judaism I never knew existed. It is one I want to practice. I did as you suggested, and sought out my local rabbi,

Rabbi K., for a meeting. At first I was intimidated. What do I say to a rabbi I did not know? But he was nice and we chatted about my experiences with Judaism and other faiths.

He knew of you and your writings, and actually used some of your poems in his services. I explained about Minyan and asked if he did anything like that. He didn't but he told me that there was a group of "new age Jews" as he called them who met at the synagogue on Saturdays before services. He invited me join them.

I have been attending the group for two months and it is wonderful. Sometimes I stay for the regular service, sometimes I don't. But I am discovering a whole new group of friends and a whole new place to explore friendship.

I remember you saying something about the power of community to lift one out of oneself. Well, that is true in my case. I still meditate and practice on my own, but now I have a weekly place to share my experiences, my setbacks and my goals. The group is supportive and energizing. We also participate in a number of social action projects sponsored by the synagogue.

I also joined the synagogue. After all, they made the group possible and I felt I owed them something. Surprisingly I find myself attending other synagogue functions as well. You were right about finding community. Thank you for encouraging me to do so. It really makes a difference.

Religion is a storehouse of human wisdom, retaining for the ages the genius of those spiritual giants who walk among us now and again. The purpose of this stored wisdom is not to supply us with the Truth, but to help us learn how to gain access to the Truth for ourselves and understand the implications of Truth for our daily lives. Unfortunately, the formalities and politics of religion often obscure its real gifts. Minyan is my way of recovering the gifts of Judaism.

I am a Jew because my primary encounter with God comes through the teachings of Torah and her sages.

I am a Jew because my articulation of my own encounter with God is expressed in the idiom of Torah and Jewish tradition.

I am a Jew because Torah speaks to me more loudly, more clearly, and more compellingly than do the other great books of divine encounter.

I am a Jew because I find within the history and culture of my people teachings, insights, and practices that bring me to proximity with God.

Proximity, not yet unity or even meeting. A Jew cannot meet God; nor can a Christian, Muslim, Hindu, Buddhist, Confucian, or Taoist. No labeled person can meet the Unlabeled and Unlabelable. Each religious tradition must be self-transcending. Each must lead its students to a point of departure and help them make the leap from tradition to Truth, God, the nondual Reality that is the Source and Substance of all things.

The experience of God does not erase my Jewishness, however. It simply reminds me that Judaism is a pointer leading me beyond itself to God. People who see religion in this way are people I call true persons of faith.

The true person of faith sees this leap not as the abandonment of her past, but as the fulfillment of her present.

The true person of faith is so secure in her tradition that she has no reason to fear learning from the insights of another.

The true person of faith seeks Truth and is not misled by ideas about Truth.

The true person of faith knows that Reality cannot be reduced to doctrine, dogma, or canon.

The true person of faith understands that the God that can be named is not the Eternal God; that the God that can be worshipped is not yet the One Beyond Thought and Label.

The true person of faith does not mistake the ism for the Is.

The true person of faith loves his tradition for what it can do and is not ashamed to admit what it cannot do.

The true person of faith knows that Reality is perceived by different peoples in different ways, and that as a human being all those ways are part of her heritage.

Thus the true person of faith seeks to learn from every tradition while being at home in her own.

If we dare to be true persons of faith, we can talk and teach, listen and learn.

If we dare to be true persons of faith, we can unite in our unknowing: doing justly, loving mercy, and walking humbly with God and each other.

Minyan is a way for me, and perhaps also for you, to become a true person of faith. I hope your experiences with these ten practices are positive ones, and I welcome hearing from you. If you would like to share your experiences with me and other like-minded people, please contact me via my website, the Virtual Yeshiva (http://www.rasheit.org/).

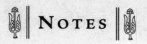

NOTES

PREFACE

[1] *Babylonian Talmud,* Sanhedrin 106b.

[2] Isaiah 6:13.

INTRODUCTION

[1] "Hear, O Israel, the Lord our God the Lord is One."

[2] Rabbi Yitzhak Epstein of Homel, cited in Arthur Green, "Hasidism: Discovery and Retreat," in *The Other Side of God,* Peter L. Berger, ed. Anchor Press. New York, 1981, p. 119.

THE TEACHING

[1] Rabbi Moshe Cordovero, *Eilima Rabati,* fol. 25a. Lvov, 1881.

[2] *Likkutei Torah,* Shir ha Shirim, Rabbi Schneur Zalman. Kehot Publication Society. Brooklyn, N.Y., 1979, fol. 41a.

[3] Rabbi Aharon HaLevi, *Sha'arei ha-Yihud ve-ha-Emunah,* portal I, chapter 2. Jerusalem, 1982.

[4] Menachem Mendel Schneerson, *Toward a Meaningful Life,* Simon Jacobson, ed. William Morrow & Company. New York, 1995, p. 215.

NECESSARY UNITY

[1] Rabbi Aharon HaLevi, *Sha'arei ha-Yihud ve-ha-Emunah,* IV, chapter 5. Jerusalem, 1982.

[2] Rabbi Aharon HaLevi, *'Avodat ha-Levi,* Va-Yehi, fol. 74a. Jerusalem, 1972.

[3] Abraham Abulafia, cited in Moshe Idel, *The Mystical Experience of Abraham Abulafia.* SUNY Press. New York, 1988, pp. 126–27.

[4] Leviticus 19:2.

WHO ARE YOU?

[1] Genesis 1:26.

⚜ NOTES ⚜

THE PRACTICE

[1] *Ayin Yaacov,* Haggigah, 24.

[2] Menachem Mendel Schneerson, *Toward a Meaningful Life.* William Morrow & Company. New York, 1995, p. 215.

THE TEN PRACTICES OF MINYAN

[1] Moses Maimonides, *Mishneh Torah,* Yesodai ha-Torah 7:4.

[2] *Babylonian Talmud,* Berachot 32b.

[3] Maimonides' commentary on Mishna Berachot 5:1.

[4] *Babylonian Talmud,* Berachot 12a–b.

[5] *Babylonian Talmud,* Berachot 28b.

[6] Psalm 84:30.

[7] Reb Nachman of Bratzlav, *Likkutei Moharan,* vol. 1, 22:10. Jerusalem, 1976.

[8] From the *Aleinu* prayer recited twice daily.

[9] Isaiah 33:18.

[10] Psalm 19:15.

[11] Psalm 37:30.

[12] Psalms 35:28, 71:24.

[13] Isaiah 38:14.

[14] Joshua 1:9.

[15] Literally: Hear, O Israel, the Lord is our God, the Lord is One. Deuteronomy 6:4.

[16] *Talmud Yerushalmi,* Tractate Berachot 1–13.

[17] Nachman of Bratzlav, *Hayei Moharan,* part 2, p. 15. Jerusalem, 1962.

[18] Psalm 150:6.

[19] Rabbi Alexander Ziskind, *Tzva'a Yekara* #34, *Yesod v'Shoresh ha-Avodah,* Jerusalem Publishing Company, 1978.

[20] Dov Baer, *Or Ha-Emet* 2b, Yahadut. Bnei Brak, Israel, 1967.

[21] Dov Baer, *Kuntres Ha-Hitpa'alut,* fol. 55 a–b, in *Likkutei Biurim.* Warsaw, 1868.

[22] Nachum of Chernobil, cited in *Hanhagot Tzaddikim,* p. 34, #5, Rabbi Y. H. Malik, ed. Jerusalem, 1976.

[23] *Mishna,* Berachot 5:l.

[24] *Babylonian Talmud,* Berachot 32b.

[25] Moses Maimonides, *Mishneh Torah,* Teffilah, 4:16.

[26] Aaron of Apt, *Keter Shem Tov.* Jerusalem, 1968, pp. 48a–48b.

[27] *Babylonian Talmud,* Bava Batra 9b.

[28] Deuteronomy 16:20.

[29] Genesis 18:25.

[30] Amos 5:24.

[31] Deuteronomy 26:12.

[32] Leviticus 19:9–10.

[33] Maimonides, *Mishneh Torah,* Laws Concerning Gifts to the Poor, 7:5.

[34] Mark Zborowski and Elizabeth Herzog, *Life Is with People.* Schocken Books. New York, 1952, pp. 193–94.

[35] *Mishna,* Pirkei Avot 2:20.

[36] *L'Yesharim Tehillah,* M. H. Kleinman. New York, 1976, p. 31.

[37] *Menorat Zahav,* N. N. HaCohen, ed. Jerusalem, p. 63.

[38] Exodus 22:21; 23:9; Leviticus 19:33–4; Deuteronomy 10:19; 23:7.

[39] *Mishna,* Pirkei Avot 1:2.

[40] *Mishna,* Pe'ah 1:1.

[41] *Babylonian Talmud,* Sukkot 49b.

[42] *Tanhumah,* Va-Yehi 3.

[43] *Ecclesiastes Rabbah* 7:1.

[44] *Babylonian Talmud,* Avodah Zarah.

[45] *Michtivei ha-Hafetz Hayim ha-Hadash,* S. Artzi, Mishor, Benei Brak. Israel, 1986, vol. 2, II, p. 85.

[46] Deuteronomy 23:20.

[47] *Babylonian Talmud,* Nedarim 39b–40a.

[48] *Babylonian Talmud,* Bava Mezia 30b.

[49] Numbers 12:13.

[50] *Babylonian Talmud,* Gittin 55b–56a.

[51] *Babylonian Talmud,* Berachot 58a.

[52] *Babylonian Talmud,* Berachot 35a.

[53] *Zohar,* Genesis, Vayashiv 183b, R. Margoliot, ed. Jerusalem, 1978.

[54] *Babylonian Talmud,* Berachot 55b.

[55] *Babylonian Talmud,* Berachot 55a.

[56] *Babylonian Talmud,* Bava Metzia 32b.

[57] *Babylonian Talmud,* Shabbat 67b.

[58] *Genesis Rabbah.*

[59] Genesis 1:29.

[60] Rashi on Genesis 1:29.

[61] Genesis 1:30.

[62] Isaiah 11:6–7.

[63] Genesis 2:15.

[64] Numbers 11:4–33.

[65] Deuteronomy 8:7–10.

[66] Amos 9:14–15.

[67] Exodus 24:9–11.

[68] Deuteronomy 20:19–20.

[69] *Babylonian Talmud,* Shabbat 67b.

[70] *Babylonian Talmud,* Kiddushin 32a.

[71] *Babylonian Talmud,* Berachot 50b.

[72] Ezekiel 18:31.

[73] *Babylonian Talmud,* Pesach 54a.

[74] *Song of Songs Rabbah* 5:2, no. 2.

[75] *Jerusalem Talmud,* Makkot 2:7, 31d.

[76] *Babylonian Talmud,* Kiddushin 40b.

[77] *Babylonian Talmud,* Shabbat 153a.

[78] *The Path of the Just,* Moshe Chayyim Luzzato, Feldheim Publishers. Jerusalem, 1987, p. 37.

[79] Leviticus 19:16.

[80] *Sefer Haredim,* Rabbi Eleazer Azikri. Jerusalem, 1984, chapter 66, #118.

[81] *Darkei Tzedek.* Jerusalem, 1965, p. 3, #15.

[82] *Seder ha-Dorot ha-Hadash.* Jerusalem, 1965, p. 59f.

[83] Genesis 2:2–3.

[84] Exodus 20:8–11.

[85] Exodus 31:13–17.

[86] Deuteronomy 5:13–15.

[87] Genesis 2:1–3.

FELLOWSHIP

[1] Elat Chayyim Retreat Center, P.O. Box 127, Woodstock, NY 12498; 800-398-2630.

[2] Heart of Stillness Retreat Center, P.O. Box 106, Jamestown, Co. 80455; 303-459-3431.

[3] Rose Mountain Center, P.O. Box 355, Las Vegas, NM 87701; 505-425-5728.

[4] ALEPH, The Alliance for Jewish Renewal, 7318 Germantown Ave., Philadelph a, PA 19119; 215-247-9800; e-mail: ALEPHajr@aol.com/.

[5] Rasheit Institute for Jewish Spirituality, P.O. Box 161238, Miami, FL 33116–1238; 305-235-1419; e-mail: rabrami@icanect.net/.

[6] National Chavurah Committee, 7318 Germantown Ave., Philadelphia, PA 19119; 215-248-9760; e-mail: 73073.601@compuserve.com/.

[7] Used with permission.

BIBLIOGRAPHY

Aaron of Apt. *Keter Shem Tov.* Jerusalem, 1968.

Afterman, Allen. *Kabbalah and Consciousness.* Sheep Meadow Press. New York, 1992.

Artzi, S. *Michtivei ha-Hafetz Hayim ha-Hadash.* Mishor. Bnei Brak, Israel, 1986.

Azikri, Eleazer. *Sefer Haredim.* Jerusalem, 1984.

Baer, Dov. *Kuntres Ha-Hitpa'alut.* Dov Baer Shneurson, in *Likkutei Biurim.* Warsaw, 1868.

———. *On Ecstasy.* Trans. Louis Jacobs. Rossel Books. Chappaqua, N.Y., 1963.

———. *Or Ha-Emet* 2b, Yahadut. Bnei Brak, Israel, 1967.

Benson, Herbert. *The Relaxation Response.* Avon. New York, 1975.

———. *Beyond the Relaxation Response.* Avon. New York, 1984.

———. *The Maximum Mind.* Avon. New York, 1987.

Boteach, Rabbi Shmuel. *Dreams.* Bash Publications. Brooklyn, N.Y., 1991.

Buxbaum, Yitzhak. *Jewish Spiritual Practices.* Jason Aronson. Northvale, N.J., 1990.

Chabib, Jacob Ibn. *Ayin Yaacov.* S. H. Glick, ed. Jerusalem, 1921.

Cordovero, Moshe. *Eilima Rabati.* Lvov, 1881.

Covitz, Joel. *Darkei Tzedek.* Jerusalem, 1965.

———. *Visions of the Night: A Study of Jewish Dream Interpretation.* Shambhala. Boston, 1990.

Elior, Rachel. *The Paradoxical Ascent to God.* SUNY Press. New York, 1993.

Green, Arthur. "Hasidism: Discovery and Retreat," in *The Other Side of God.* Peter L. Berger, ed. Anchor Press. New York, 1981.

———. *Seek My Face, Speak My Name.* Jason Aronson. Northvale, N.J., 1992.

Green, Arthur, and Barry W. Holtz. *Your Word Is Fire.* Jewish Lights Publishing. Woodstock, Vt., 1993.

HaCohen, N. N. *Menorat Zahav.* Jerusalem, n.d.

HaLevi, Aharon. *Avodat ha-Levi.* Jerusalem, 1972.

———. *Sha'arei ha-Yihud ve-ha-Emunah.* Jerusalem, 1982.

Harris, Monford. *Studies in Jewish Dream Interpretation.* Jason Aronson. Northvale, N.J., 1994.

Idel, Moshe. *The Mystical Experience of Abraham Abulafia.* SUNY Press. New York, 1988.

———. *Studies in Ecstatic Kabbalah.* SUNY Press. New York, 1988.

Idel, Moshe, and Bernard McGinn, eds. *Mystical Union in Judaism, Christianity and Islam.* Continuum. New York, 1996.

Jacobs, Louis. *Jewish Mystical Testimonies.* Schocken Books. New York, 1976.

———. *Holy Living.* Jason Aronson. Northvale, N.J., 1990.

Kaplan, Aryeh. *Meditation and the Bible.* Samuel Weiser. New York, 1978.

———. *Meditation and the Kabbalah.* Samuel Weiser. New York, 1982.

———. *Jewish Meditation.* Schocken Books. New York, 1985.

Kravitz, Leonard, and Kerry Olitsky, trans. and eds. *The Journey of the Soul.* Jason Aronson. Northvale, N.J., 1996.

L'Yesharim Tehillah. M. H. Kleinman. New York, 1976.

Luzzatto, Moshe Chayim. *The Path of the Just.* Trans. Yaakov Feldman. Jason Aronson. Northvale, N.J., 1996.

Maimonides, Moshe. *Mishneh Torah.*

Malik, Y. H. *Hanhagot Tzaddikim.* Jerusalem, 1976.

Mindel, Nissan. *The Philosophy of Chabad.* Kehot Publication Society. Brooklyn, N.Y., 1973.

Nachman of Bratzlav. *Likkutei Moharan.* Jerusalem, 1976.

———. *Outpouring of the Soul.* Trans. Aryeh Kaplan. Breslov Research Institute. New York, 1980.

———. *Advice.* Breslov Research Institute. New York, 1983.

Newman, Louis I. *Hasidic Anthology.* Schocken Books. New York, 1972.

Paquda, Bahya Ibn. *Duties of the Heart.* Trans. Yaakov Feldman. Jason Aronson. Northvale, N.J., 1996.

Raz, Simcha. *The Sayings of Menahem Mendel of Kotsk.* Jason Aronson, Northvale, N.J., 1995.

Schachter-Shalomi, Zalman Meshullam. *Spiritual Intimacy.* Jason Aronson. Northvale, N.J., 1991.

Schneerson, Menachem M. *On the Essence of Chassidus.* Kehot Publication Society Brooklyn, N.Y., 1986.

———. *Toward a Meaningful Life,* Simon Jacobson, ed. William Morrow & Company. New York, 1995.

Schneerson, Shalom DovBer. *To Know God.* Kehot Publication Society. Brooklyn, N.Y., 1993.

Schochet, Jacob Immanuel. *Mystical Concepts in Chassidism.* Kehot Publication Society. Brooklyn, N.Y., 1988.

Scholem, Gershom. *The Messianic Idea in Judaism.* Schocken Books, New York, 1972

———. "Devekut, or Communion with God," in *Essential Papers on Hasidism,* Gershon David Hundert, ed. NYU Press. New York, 1991.

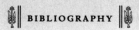 BIBLIOGRAPHY

Schwartz, Richard H. *Seder ha-Dorot ha-Hadash.* Jerusalem, 1965.

———. *Judaism and Vegetarianism.* Micah Publications. Marblehead, Mass., 1988.

Shapiro, Rami M. *Wisdom of the Jewish Sages.* Bell Tower. New York, 1993.

Sperling, Harry, and Maurice Simon. *Zohar.* Soncino Press. New York, 1970.

Steinsaltz, Adin. *The Thirteen Petalled Rose.* Jason Aronson. Northvale, N.J., 1992.

Telushkin, Joseph. *Jewish Literacy.* William Morrow & Co. New York, 1991.

Uffenheimer, Rivka Schatz. *Hasidism as Mysticism.* Magnes. Princeton, N.J., 1993.

Verman, Mark. *The Books of Contemplation: Medieval Jewish Mystical Sources.* SUNY Press. New York, 1992.

Zalman, Shneur. *Likkutei Torah.* Kehot Publication Society. Brooklyn, N.Y., 1979.

———. *To Touch the Divine.* Merkos L'Inyonei Chinuch. Brooklyn, N.Y., 1989.

Zborowski, Mark, and Elizabeth Herzog. *Life Is with People.* Schocken Books. New York, 1952.

———. *Zohar,* R. Margoliot, ed. Jerusalem, 1978.

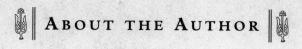

ABOUT THE AUTHOR

Rami Shapiro, rabbi and storyteller of Temple Beth Or in Miami, Florida, is an award-winning poet and essayist, whose liturgical poems are used in prayer services throughout North America. He has published more than a dozen books of poetry, liturgy, stories, and nonfiction. Rabbi Shapiro holds a doctoral degree in religious studies and lectures widely on contemporary Jewish spirituality. He is the director of the Rasheit Institute for Jewish Spirituality in Miami.